A PUBLIC SCHOOL OF YOUR OWN

A Public School of Your Own

Your Guide to Creating and Running a Charter School

Catherine Blakemore

A-PP

Adams-Pomeroy Press

Golden, Colorado

Published by:

A-PP   Adams-Pomeroy Press
        P.O. Box 26
        Wheat Ridge, Colorado 80034-0026

Printed in the United States of America
First Printing 1998

Cover and book design by Paulette Livers Lambert

Publisher's Cataloging-in-Publication
(Provided by Quality Books, Inc.)

Blakemore, Catherine.
    A public school of your own : your guide to
    creating and running a charter school / Catherine
    Blakemore. -- 1st ed.
        p. cm.
    Includes bibliographical references and index.
    Preassigned LCCN: 97-77067
    ISBN: 0-9661009-1-3

    1. Charter schools.   I. Title.

LB2806.36.B53 1998   371'.04
                                QBI97-41352

CONTENTS

STEPPING STONE 8

*Establish Communication Procedures
and Make Effective Communication
a Continuing Priority*   **137**

Intra-school Communication • School–Parent
Communication • School–Community Communication •
School–Sponsoring Agency Communication

STEPPING STONE 9

*Institute a Management System That Is
Role-Specific, Time-Efficient, People-
Friendly, and Change-Responsive*   **145**

Role-Specific • Time-Efficient • People-Friendly
• Change-Responsive

STEPPING STONE 10

*Actively Pursue New Funding Sources
and Arrangements*   **153**

Funding Sources • Funding Arrangements

STEPPING STONE 11

*Base Decisions at Every Level on
the Criterion: "This School Is for
the Students."*   **159**

Measures of Success • Students • Parents •
Staff/Administrator • Governing Board • Policy Decisions

STEPPING STONE 12
....

List of Tables

ACKNOWLEDGMENTS

Like a charter school, this book could not have been created by one person alone. Although I take full responsibility for its contents, I am indebted to the contributions of many others.

In doing the research for this book, I benefited immeasurably from my interviews with Mary Lyn Ballantine, Cordia Booth, Rexford Brown, Sarah Brunnig, Sandra Elliott, Robert Hamilton-Pennell, Carol Irwin, Ginny Jaramillo, Mark Levine, Meera Mani, Judy Mikulas, Sam Pantleo, Ray Rodriguez, and Dave Van Manen. I would like to thank each of them for sharing their experiences and insights.

The extensive input which I received as to content, format, and editorial change has helped make this book a better one. I greatly appreciate the time spent and thoughtful comments provided by those who reviewed the first draft of my manuscript: Elizabeth Blakemore, Karen Byars, Carolyn DeRaad, Bay Jackson, Moe Keller, Meera Mani, Sharon Simas, Belinda Smiley, Gail Van Hove, and James Weigel.

I would like to thank Elizabeth Blakemore also for the invaluable advice, feedback, and support which she provided throughout the writing of this book.

During the book's final stages of preparation, I was fortunate to draw upon Paulette Livers Lambert's expertise in cover and interior design and Mary Brinkopf's proofreading skills. My thanks to both of them.

The suggestions stemming from my membership in SPAN (Small Publishers Association of North America) and CIPA (Colorado Independent Publishers Association) have also been most helpful in making the production of this book a reality.

Finally, a thank you to the many pioneers in the charter school movement: charter school developers, administrators, staff, governing board members, parents, and students; school district board members and staff; state department of education personnel; governors; legislators; researchers; and other charter school supporters. It is upon your experiences that this book is based. It is for you and for those who will follow you that this book is written.

INTRODUCTION

The Charter School Journey

"This reform is all about making little people a part of the whole delivery package for education." So the charter school movement was described by Cordia Booth, driving force behind the proposed Thurgood Marshall Charter Middle School in Denver, Colorado.

Thurgood Marshall was initially proposed as a charter school for the 1994–95 school year. Despite opposition from her school district, which has even contested the jurisdiction of the state board of education, Booth is still pushing her proposal. It is her belief in "people that now have no say in making changes that count" and her determination "to see it through" that make Booth an embodiment of the charter school movement (Interview, 1996).

Booth's experience has been unusual. As of September 1997 in the United States there were 787 charter schools operating and an additional 68 approved for the 1997-98 school year (Center for Education Reform, 1997a). Compared with Booth's itinerary, the paths to these charter schools were generally more direct, but the organizers of these schools, as well as those organizers whose proposals were turned down, reflect her belief in charter schools. What exactly is the charter school in which they believe, the destination of their journeys?

THE DESTINATION

There are numerous definitions of a charter school. For readers of this book, a charter school is defined as follows: *A*

*charter school is a **public school** of **choice** which is authorized by*
***state statute** and which is **established by** and operates under the*
*terms of a **charter** granted to **school organizers** by a **public***
sponsoring agency** to whom the school is thereafter **account-
***able**.* To clarify this definition, let us look at the bold itali-
cized words.

Public school

Perhaps the most common misconception about charter
schools is that they are private schools. In truth, probably the
most important element of a charter school is that it is public.
To the taxpayers this means that it is financed largely by
their tax dollars. To the school district this means that the
charter school within its boundaries is supported by public
school funds. To parents this means that the school is nondiscriminatory in its admission policy, is open to all students
within a specified area, does not charge tuition, and will not
teach religion. To the school this means that it is assured of a
certain level of public funding in return for operating as a
public institution that is subject to all applicable federal laws
and to those applicable state laws from which it has not been
granted waivers.

Choice

If the most important feature of a charter school is that it
is public, arguably the second most important characteristic
is choice. Charter school organizers make the choice to establish a charter school. They decide what kind of school they
want. They determine the school's educational program;
define the roles of students, parents, staff, administrator, and
governing board; select a site; determine their budget; enlist
community support; and prepare an application. In effect,

they work towards establishing a public school of their own. Once their application is approved, they will be joined by the parents, students, staff, administrator, and governing board members who choose to become part of this particular school because they believe in its mission and program. Although the degree of school autonomy will vary according to state legislation and the terms of the charter, together they will exercise choice in making the major and minor decisions that will make their school a reality. As time passes, some individuals will choose to leave, others will choose to sign on, and the school will continue to make choices that shape both its present and its future.

State statute

Charter schools can be established only in those states which have enacted legislation authorizing their existence. This legislation, which varies by state, includes provisions governing their establishment, legal status, exemption from various regulations, funding, operation, and accountability and may limit the number of charters granted.

Charter

The legal instrument establishing a charter school is its charter. A charter is a contract entered into by a governmental authority and an individual or group which establishes an organization and grants it rights and privileges (*Webster's Encyclopedic Unabridged Dictionary of the English Language,* 1989, p. 249). Under each state's charter school law a charter application is to cover certain specific areas. The charter sets forth the terms under which the school is to operate and be accountable and the duration of the charter.

School organizers

The organizers are the individuals (or individual) who propose a charter school and submit a charter school application to a sponsoring agency. Depending on the state's charter school law, organizers may be:

- parents,
- teachers,
- community members,
- a university or college,
- a nonsectarian entity,
- an existing public school,
- part of an existing public school,
- a private or independent school,
- a school district employees group,
- a city or parish school system,
- a local school board,
- an educational services contractor,
- a business or corporate entity,
- a nonprofit organization, and/or
- a governmental entity (Vergari and Mintrom, 1996).

Public sponsoring agency

The sponsoring agency grants, revokes, and renews charters and oversees each charter school's performance. Again, depending upon the state's statute, sponsoring agencies may be:

- the commissioner of education,
- a local school board,
- a local school committee,
- an intermediate school board,
- a regional school board,
- the state board of education,

- the state superintendent,
- a public charter school board,
- the board of regents,
- a community college, and/or
- a state public university (Vergari and Mintrom, 1996).

Accountability

A charter's accountability to its sponsoring agency usually focuses on the progress it has made towards meeting the goals set forth in its charter and on its compliance with all applicable laws. The school will also be economically accountable, that is, demonstrating financial viability.

THE SCOUTING REPORT

How many pioneers are already making the charter school journey and what accounts are they sending back? According to Louann A. Bierlein, charter school authority and education policy adviser to the Governor of Louisiana, "Charter schools may be the most vibrant force in American education today" (U.S. Congress, 1997, p. 138). Her statement reflects in part the rapid growth of the charter school movement.

The first charter school legislation was enacted in Minnesota in 1991, and in September 1992 City Academy in St. Paul opened its doors as the nation's first charter school. In 1992 California became the second state to authorize charter schools. Six states enacted charter school legislation in 1993, three more joined the movement in 1994, eight states became charter school states in 1995, and in 1996 six additional states and the District of Columbia adopted charter school statutes. As of July 1997 twenty-nine states plus the District of Columbia had become charter school states. In November 1996 105,127 students were enrolled in charter schools (Dale, 1996).

President Clinton has urged an increase in the number of charter schools (Clinton, 1997), and the charter school movement has received bipartisan support. However, there has been opposition to the movement, primarily among school districts, teacher unions, and others who see charter schools as a threat to current public school systems.

Further, the path to establishing charter schools has not been easy. Major obstacles have faced charter schools, especially in the areas of funding (particularly capital and start-up costs), the securing of adequate facilities, governance, and the provision of special education services. Indeed, we are still awaiting a conclusive charter school scouting report. One of the most crucial measures of success is student performance. Although individual charter schools have achieved varying degrees of success on this measure, there is not yet sufficient data for a definitive assessment. However, a 1997 Hudson Institute report has pointed out, "While there aren't a lot of comparable test scores as of yet, early signs are promising" (Vanourek et al., 1997b, p. 6).

There are other indications of charter school success. In his book on charter schools Joe Nathan reported, "Charter schools can have a positive effect on student achievement, attendance, and attitude" (1996, p. 167).

Charter schools have offered a wide range of curricula, have elicited strong parent involvement, and have been innovative in their educational programs and their management (Finn, Manno, and Bierlein, 1996, pp. 3-4).

The Hudson Institute concluded from its parent, student, and teacher surveys: "These surveys paint a statistical portrait that is compelling: there are striking levels of satisfaction among all the constituents of charter schools, their focus is on education (without frills), their students are flourishing academically, and they are havens for children—of all races, backgrounds, and abilities—who were not thriving in conventional schools" (Vanourek et al., 1997a, p. 9).

Testifying before the House Subcommittee on Early Childhood, Youth and Families, Scott W. Hamilton, Associate Commissioner for Charter Schools in Massachusetts, stated, "Mr. Chairman, the charter school experience in Massachusetts has been very positive" (U.S. Congress, 1997, p. 227).

To cite one other assessment: "After careful evaluation, the Little Hoover Commission believes charter schools are a positive force in today's education system. There is no claim that the charter school movement is a panacea for all the ills of public schools. But it is a powerful tool that is unleashing creative energy. The beneficiaries are California's children" (1996, p. 99).

THE STEPPING STONES

A charter school offers you the opportunity to give children the type of education in which you believe. Would you, the reader, one of the "little people", really be able to pull it off? How would you go about creating and running the charter school that will turn your ideas into reality?

If you are currently involved with a charter school, if you are preparing a charter proposal, if you are merely intrigued by the possibilities a charter school offers—this book is written for you.

It offers to those of you residing in states now having or about to have charter school statutes a route to the creation and running of a charter school.

TABLE 1	*Twelve Stepping Stones*

1. Explore your options
2. Create an organizing committee which is broad-based in composition, narrowly-focused in educational mission, and strongly committed to that mission
3. Maximize your organizing committee's utilization of the Four E's: expertise, efficiency, effectiveness, and enterprise
4. Develop a detailed plan for your school's operation and incorporate all or part of it into your application
5. If your application is rejected, activate Plan B; if approved, negotiate a charter which meets your priorities and prepare for start-up
6. Create a learning/working environment which is comfortable, supportive, challenging, rewarding, and enjoyable
7. Foster a sense of school ownership in your students, your parents, your staff, your administrator, and your governing board
8. Establish communication procedures and make effective communication a continuing priority
9. Institute a management system that is role-specific, time-efficient, people-friendly, and change-responsive
10. Actively pursue new funding sources and arrangements
11. Base decisions at every level on the criterion: "This school is for the students."
12. Anticipate that each day will be different: new travelers, new terrain, new sunrises, and new sunsets

Table 1 presents the twelve stepping stones which will guide you on your charter school journey. Regardless of the type of school you wish to establish or are currently operating, regardless of your state's charter school law, and regardless of whether you have experience with charter schools or are a novice, these stepping stones will help lead your way.

Each of this book's chapters presents and elaborates upon one of the stepping stones. If you are just starting out in the charter school field, read them all. If you already are involved with a charter school, begin your reading with Stepping Stone 3. Although Stepping Stones 3, 4, and 5 relate specifically to the period before a school's start-up, they contain information useful to an operating school.

This book will not be the only guide you will need on your journey. Appendix C refers you to other resources, and throughout the book you will be advised to secure particular types of assistance and to check out the specific requirements in your state.

A major roadblock facing charter school developers has been the lack of know-how and guidance. This guidebook has been written to help fill that void—to make your journey a smoother one.

Stepping Stone 1

Explore Your Options

"Not for the faint-hearted"—this advice from charter school administrator Rexford Brown (Interview, 1997) should be posted at the trailhead of each charter school journey. Exhausting and exhilarating, emotionally-draining and emotionally-fulfilling, your involvement in creating and running a charter school will be one of the most demanding and rewarding experiences of your life. Like parenthood, it requires a sustained commitment and on-the-job learning. And, like parenthood, you don't know what you're getting into until you've been through it.

With the assistance of the twelve stepping stones and of those who have preceded you, you will be able to follow some guideposts on your journey. Yet, the charter school movement is young and each charter school experience unique. You will be one of the pioneers, exploring largely virgin territory, taking risks, and making your own discoveries. Is the charter school path for you? Before you decide to take it, look at your reasons and investigate the other options.

YOUR REASONS
....

The reasons for establishing a charter school are legion—
Parent:
- You would like your child to have a happy, successful school experience.
- You would like your child's school to emphasize academic content/the learning process.

- You would like your child's school to impose a great/small amount of discipline.
- Your child needs a school which responds to his/her needs.
- Your child needs good teachers.
- Your child needs to be prepared for college.
- Your child needs academic challenge/support.
- You want to play a major role in your child's education.
- You would like your child to be in a small class in which he/she would receive individual attention.
- You would like a school with a strong parent-teacher organization.
- Your child is in a good school, but you feel that a different educational approach would better suit his/her learning style.
- Your child needs a school with high expectations and many educational opportunities.
- You would like a school in which teachers devote time to all children, not just those with problems.
- You would like a school which meets the needs of your child who has an IEP or is at-risk.
- You would like a safe school.
- You would like a school which addresses the drug problem.
- You would like an elementary school which will provide a good education for your preschool-aged child.
- Your child is in a Montessori preschool and you would like him/her to continue in a Montessori school.
- You would like your home school which is part of a public education system to be free of unrealistic requirements.

Teacher:
- You would like to teach in a school which gives you authority and respect.
- You would love to have the opportunity to innovate.
- You would like class sizes small enough to give the children the individual attention they need.
- You would like to help children who have had unsuccessful school experiences and/or are at-risk.
- You would like to teach in a school in which your educational approach matches that of the principal and the staff.
- Through reading, observation, and/or personal experience, you have developed an educational philosophy which you would like to implement.
- A group of teachers who generally share your views have played around with the idea of starting their own school.
- A group of teachers in your public school would like to convert your school into a charter school that would be innovative and responsive to the community's needs.

Administrator:
- You would like the opportunity to implement reforms.
- You would like to provide students, parents and teachers with a choice of educational programs.
- You would like to boost students' standardized test scores.
- As the administrator of a private school, you would like to promote reform in your school district by converting your school to a charter school.

Community:

• You would like your rural community to have its own school so that students will not have long bus rides.

• As a city council member, you would like to encourage the development of an economically-stagnant portion of your city by developing a school which would attract young families.

• As the manager of a business, you would like to be able to hire high school graduates who are technically-competent and/or computer-literate.

• As a college faculty member, you would like to teach freshmen who are prepared for college-level work.

• You would like a school in your community for students who have dropped out or are potential dropouts.

• You would like an alternative educational option in your community.

• You would like your community to meet the needs of those students who are unable to get into your district's alternative schools because of their long waiting lists.

These are just some of the reasons for considering the establishment of a charter school. What are yours? Take the time to write out your reasons, express them as goals, and prioritize them.

Once you have determined your goals, you will be better able to evaluate which options best meet these goals within your individual parameters. Factor in such items as the time you are willing to commit, the money you can spend, the ideas you would like to contribute, your comfort level in being a leader or a participant, your family and other responsibilities—and explore the options.

YOUR OPTIONS
· ·

Your current school

Whether you are a parent, a teacher, or an administrator making changes in your current school is the least disruptive option. If a parent, your child will not have to leave familiar surroundings and make the transition to a new school. If a teacher or administrator, you will not have to go through the turmoil of changing jobs.

What are the possibilities for real change at your school? Does your district have the policy of moving administrators after a few years? Is your administrator near the retirement age? Are some of the "problem teachers" near the retirement age? Will the election of a new school board or the selection of a new superintendent lend more support to your reform efforts?

Do many parents/teachers share your vision? Can they join together to make a difference? Do you have a site-based advisory or management committee at your school and does it have a voice?

Is there any chance of your school receiving additional funds because of the current crowding or its high number of low income or LEP (limited-English proficient) students? Is your school willing to make greater use of classroom volunteers?

As a parent, have you checked out the teachers in the upper grades of your child's school? Is there any chance that you can switch your child to a different class/request a specific teacher for the next year?

In short, can enough changes be made to make your current school an acceptable option?

A different public school

Your state or your school district may have an open enrollment policy whereby you can enroll your child in any public school provided that the school has space and you furnish the transportation.

If so, visit other schools, talk to the principals, and, if you are interested, speak to parents with children in the school. See if one of these schools would be better for your child. Remember that changing schools will mean that your child will not be attending school with neighborhood friends. On the other hand, your child will have the opportunity to make a new start.

Transportation will probably be an issue. If you live in an urban area and your child is old enough, perhaps public transportation is a possibility. If you can locate a good school near your job, your transportation problem will be minimized.

You may discover that other parents at your school are seeking a different educational program and will join you in changing schools. This may make the transition to the new school an easier one for your child, and you can alleviate your transportation problems by forming a car pool.

Remember that if your child goes to an after-school baby-sitter or day care center, different arrangements may have to be made. See whether the new school has an extended-day program. If you have an older child who is into athletics, you will need to see whether transfer students are eligible to participate in interscholastic sports.

If you are a teacher or administrator, network with others to discover which schools are more attuned to your needs. Are there any job openings at these schools? Keep on top of employment opportunities.

An alternative school

Whether they're called focus schools, magnet schools, alternative schools, pilot schools or some other name, your school district may include schools with distinctive approaches that are open to children district-wide on a voluntary basis. Although alternative schools do not have the degree of autonomy of charter schools, they do offer parents the opportunity for school choice.

Are any of these schools appealing to you? If so, check to see whether there are any entrance qualifications, whether the school district provides transportation, whether (if you do not reside in the district) they permit out-of-district enrollment, and, the biggie, whether the length of their waiting list precludes your child from ever getting in.

Some school districts are responding to the movement for school choice, whether through establishing alternative schools or approving charter school applications. Check to see whether your district is planning any new alternative schools. If there is a long waiting list at the alternative school you have selected, you may be assured that a large number of parents share your educational views and are similarly frustrated in getting their children into the school of their choice. Consider joining with them to put pressure on the district to open an additional alternative school.

With the movement towards more alternative schools, teachers and administrators also have a greater chance of finding a school which matches their educational philosophy and approach.

An existing or soon-to-exist charter school

Perhaps an existing charter school will best suit your needs. Although the number of charter schools is still limited, you may live in or near a school district which has the school for you or your child. Ask your school district or your state department of education whether any charter applications have been approved, submitted, or are planned.

Determine whether these schools will provide the educational alternative you are seeking. Visit existing schools, check out their track records, and contact organizers of schools which are not yet operational. Find out how students are selected, whether through a waiting list or by lottery, and what chance your child has of enrolling. Find out whether transportation is provided and determine what involvement would be required or expected of you as a parent.

If you are a teacher or administrator, see if there are any job openings. Be aware that a charter school may have a large number of applicants for each position. Get information on the charter school's salaries and job benefits. Determine whether you would be a school district employee and how employment at a charter school would affect your tenure and ability to return to school district employment. Carefully evaluate the benefits of working in a school whose educational philosophy and approach match your own versus the probably intense workload.

It is much easier to join a charter school than to be involved in creating one. Consider yourself fortunate if there is an existing or soon-to-exist charter school which meets your needs.

A private school

Another option is a private school. Parents will pay for an education for their children only if they feel that a private school offers their children something not available in the public school system. This may be a particular curriculum, strong academic standards, fewer problem children, more personalized attention, religious training, a high college acceptance rate, or some other attribute.

On the other hand, you may find it impossible or undesirable to enroll your child in a private school because of its long waiting list, restrictive entry standards, religious bent, elitist demographics, your commitment to public education, and, of course, the high tuition.

If you are a teacher or administrator seeking to teach in a private school, here again investigate the salary and benefits as well as the extent of your authority.

If charter schools are not an option in your state, or even if they are, you may choose to establish a private school. You will be following a more traditional path without all the ambiguities associated with the incipient charter school movement. You will not have to worry about establishing relationships with and being accountable to a sponsoring agency. You will be in control.

With this control comes the financial risk of running your own business. You must have the financial resources to start your own school. You must be able to please parents, to attract and keep students, and to run an efficient business. In many ways, setting up a private school is similar to setting up a charter school. Indeed, once Colorado had passed its charter school legislation, The Connect School in Pueblo was quickly able to become the state's first charter school because it had already been planned as a private school. As a charter school, it is able to serve as a research laboratory for its school district (Interview with Mikulas, 1996).

A home school

Being in control is probably the important advantage of a home school. When you have a home school, you are in charge of the program, whether your emphasis is the educational philosophy of John Holt or moral and character development. You can individualize your teaching, allowing children to pursue their interests and letting them advance at their own pace. There is no need for written tests as you are well aware of your children's progress. Your time schedule can be flexible, giving children time to pursue projects without arbitrary schedule limitations and to skip classes when they are sick. For some parents, home schooling is a means of avoiding public school teaching which is contrary to their convictions. For some, a home school is the means of sparing their children a long and tiring commute. For those parents whose jobs require frequent travel, home schooling allows their children to accompany them (Interviews with Brunnig and Van Manen, 1997).

There is some question as to whether the potential lack of socialization is an advantage or disadvantage of home schools. Some parents want their children to be isolated from what they regard as a negative school environment. Some actively seek out the company of other home-schooled children (Interview with Brunnig, 1997). Some make sure that their children are "not cloistered at home", but "use the community as a classroom" (Interview with Van Manen, 1997).

There are, however, definite challenges in home schooling. One is the interruptions which can be caused by your family's younger children. Another is the need to either purchase textbooks or develop your own curriculum. This can be a problem especially when your children are older and they pursue more academically advanced subjects. It is difficult for parents to keep up with, let alone challenge, these children and almost impossible for them to provide such resources as a science laboratory (Interview with Brunnig, 1997).

Money and time can be another difficulty. Not only must you spend money for school materials, but in some cases parents must forgo both the satisfaction and earnings of a career.

Many families do not have the interest, time, or financial resources to educate their children at home.

A new charter school

Is establishment of a charter school an option for you? The answer to this question depends to a great extent on where you live. Table 2 lists those states which had adopted charter school laws as of July 1997. Other states are considering legislation. If your state is not on this list, contact your state department of education or state legislature to learn about the passage or progress of charter school legislation.

That your state has legislation authorizing charter schools doesn't mean that establishing a charter school is a viable option. There is great variation in the strength of the statutes which have been enacted.

Researchers specializing in charter schools have established various standards for judging the strength of charter school legislation. Mark Buechler has used a set of ten criteria in ranking those state laws enacted through 1996 from strongest (1) to weakest (26) (Center for Education Reform, 1997b). (See Table 2.)

You can perceive some of the effects of this variation by further examining Table 2. Note that Arizona, whose charter school legislation dates from 1994, had 247 operating charter schools in September 1997, whereas Kansas, with legislation enacted in that same year, had only one charter school in operation. In examining the table, be sure that you take into account the year of the first statute. Those states that enacted legislation more recently cannot be expected to have a high number of charter schools.

The number of operating schools does not tell the whole story. In some states there is a cap on charter schools. For instance, New Mexico has already met its limit, five charter

Table 2	Charter School States, July 1997		
State	Year of First Law	Ranking by Strength of Law	Number of Operating Charter Schools, September 1997
Alaska	1995	19	15
Arizona	1994	1	247
Arkansas	1995	26	0
California	1992	13	128
Colorado	1993	15	49
Connecticut	1996	17	12
Delaware	1995	4	3
District of Columbia	1996	2	3
Florida	1996	6	34
Georgia	1993	25	21
Hawaii	1994	24	2
Illinois	1996	9	8
Kansas	1994	22	1
Louisiana	1995	16	6
Massachusetts	1993	7	23
Michigan	1993	3	110
Minnesota	1991	10	29
Mississippi	1997		0
Nevada	1997		0
New Hampshire	1995	11	0
New Jersey	1996	12	13
New Mexico	1993	23	5
North Carolina	1996	5	34
Ohio	1997		0
Pennsylvania	1997		6
Rhode Island	1995	20	1
South Carolina	1996	8	1
Texas	1995	14	19
Wisconsin	1993	18	17
Wyoming	1995	21	0
			787

Source: Center for Education Reform, 1997a; Center for Education Reform, 1997b; "National News Notes," 1997, p. 6.

schools. California has not only met, but exceeded its cap of 100 schools because its state board of education has exercised its authority to grant waivers to the limitation. Some states such as Colorado and Minnesota have raised their initial caps (Vergari and Mintrom, 1996).

You will need not only to check whether there are limits on the number of charter schools allowed, but also whether your state allows only conversions of existing public schools, whether private schools may be converted to charter schools, whether charter schools can be started by for-profit companies, and whether charter schools can be home-based. There are numerous variations in other areas, including funding, number of sponsoring agencies, legal status, etc. Check the most recent edition of Vergari and Mintrom's *Charter Schools Laws across the United States*, which summarizes key components of each state's legislation.

Once you have an idea of the prospects of establishing a charter school in your state, determine whether the state's charter schools can be, or indeed, must be, sponsored by school districts. If so, it is important to determine your district's receptivity to charter applications. Within the same state there is likely to be a continuum of supportive/reluctant school districts.

Table 3 shows the Colorado fall 1996 school membership (enrollment) of its fourteen most populous school districts, the number of charter schools which were operational in those districts at that time, and the same data for those smaller districts having charter schools.

As can be seen, the Denver Public School District with an enrollment of 66,331 students had the same number of charter schools (2) as did Pueblo County Rural District 70 with an enrollment of 5,524 and Durango 9-R with a 4,729 student enrollment. Two of the fourteen most populous school

Table 3
Number of Operating Charter Schools in Colorado's Fourteen Most Populous School Districts and in Those Smaller School Districts Which Have Charter Schools, Fall 1997

School District	Public School Membership Fall 1996	Number of Charter Schools 9/18/97
Jefferson County R-1	86,670	8
Denver County 1	66,331	2
Cherry Creek 5	37,128	1
Colorado Springs 11	33,175	4
Adams-Arapahoe 28J	28,492	0
Boulder Valley RE-2	25,648	2
Northglenn-Thornton 12	25,604	3
Douglas County RE-1	24,495	6
Poudre R-1	21,922	1
Mesa County Valley 51	19,049	0
Pueblo City 60	18,100	2
St. Vrain Valley RE1J	17,459	1
Littleton 6	16,044	1
Academy 20	14,715	1
Greeley 6	13,662	2
Westminster 50	11,360	1
Pueblo County Rural 70	5,524	2
Durango 9-R	4,729	2
Roaring Fork RE-1	4,729	1
Canon City RE-1	4,100	1
Eagle County RE 50	3,954	1
Lewis-Palmer 38	3,787	1
Montezuma-Cortez RE-1	3,541	1
Cheyenne Mountain 12	3,458	1
Summit RE-1	2,380	1
Elizabeth C-1	2,339	1
Gunnison Watershed RE1J	1,645	1
Park County RE-2	600	1
Moffat 2	206	1

Source: Colorado Department of Education, 1996, pp. 1-5; Windler, 1997, Appendix B.

districts had no charter schools, including the city of Aurora's district (Adams-Arapahoe 28J), which had an enrollment of more than 28,000. On the other hand, some of the state's smallest school districts had charter schools.

If your state's charter school law has been in effect for several years, the number of charter schools operating in your district may be a good weather vane of your district's willingness to approve charter schools. You should also check as to how many applications have been rejected and how many have received approval or preliminary approval for a future school year. In some cases, applications are approved without sufficient funding or prior to finding a site and the school never becomes operational. Talk to charter school staff in your state department of education to get a feel as to the potential of charter school applications in your district and state.

If you are seriously considering establishing a charter school, take the time to get an overview of the charter school movement by reading a book or report such as Nathan's *Charter Schools: Creating Hope and Opportunity for American Education* or Finn, Manno, and Bierlein's *Charter Schools in Action: What Have We Learned?* As you read the stepping stones presented in this book, keep in mind that a how-to book tries to look at possible obstacles. Don't be intimidated by the amount of know-how and skills needed to create and run a charter school. These should come from your whole team, not just from you personally.

Finally, soul-search. In the context of what you have learned and of your personal or your organization's situation, is this the best choice for you?

If your answer is yes, you are about to embark on a most exciting and challenging journey. You have just become a turn-of-the-century pioneer!

Stepping Stone 2

....

Create an Organizing Committee Which Is Broad-Based in Composition, Narrowly-Focused in Educational Mission, and Strongly Committed to That Mission

"'You've got to know in your heart that this is really what you want to do; and the people around you have to feel that way, too. Form a core group, and take the time to get to know each other before you embark on this, because it really is a journey.'" Such was the advice given at a 1995 charter school conference in Franklin, Massachusetts by Kristen McCormack of the Neighborhood House Charter School of Dorchester (Pioneer Institute for Public Policy Research, 1996, p. viii-3).

You cannot do it alone. Once you have decided that you are interested in establishing a charter school, your first step will be finding those who share your educational views and want to join you in creating the school.

FINDING OTHERS OF LIKE PERSUASION
....

Perhaps you have come up with your charter school idea on your own and will need to find partners immediately. On the other hand, your interest in starting a charter school may have been sparked by a discussion with other parents or teachers who would like to explore the feasibility of creating a "from-scratch" school or converting your existing school to charter status. You may already have a nucleus group.

During the first couple of meetings you may want to keep your group small as your intentions are as yet uncertain and nebulous. However, very soon you will need to expand your organizing group so that it includes parents, teachers, community members, an attorney, and a business manager or accountant. If your school will be for older children, also consider including potential students.

How do you locate those who could become part of your group? Start out by contacting relatives, friends, and acquaintances to see if they or someone they know might be interested in joining with you. Talk to parents and/or teachers at your children's current school, parents at your children's soccer games or other activities, acquaintances in your aerobics class or running group, your co-workers, members of your church, and contacts at professional organizations, tenant associations, craft classes, or any other groups to which you belong. If you are a teacher, you may know educators who share your philosophy as well as parents who are looking for an alternative. Get your family and friends to do similar networking. Remember that word-of-mouth is one of the most effective ways of finding committee members.

If there is a similar alternative or charter school in your district which has a long waiting list, you can be assured that there are other parents who share your educational views and are seeking the kind of school you want for their children. There may well be some among them who would join with you in setting up a new charter school.

Likewise, if there are preschools or kindergartens based on your educational philosophy, e.g., Montessori or Waldorf, you have a real possibility of finding partners for your venture. Parents of soon-to-be graduates of these schools may be interested in having their children continue to receive the same type of education. Even if you are seeking to establish a Montessori school for the middle grades, these parents of young children may well have older children whom they would like to enroll in a Montessori school.

You can ask your local newspaper to run notices of your organizational meetings, inviting anyone interested in participating. At this point, your description of the possible school will be very brief, e.g., a middle school based on hands-on learning. You may also post flyers at places frequented by families, such as supermarkets, libraries, and toy stores.

It is likely that, especially initially, you will add new members to your committee and lose others. This is not only to be expected, but even welcomed. It is important that those who do not believe strongly in the school's philosophy or are reluctant to make an extensive contribution of their time and effort be comfortable in deciding to leave the committee. Your committee needs to be composed of those who are in it for the long haul.

SETTING UP INITIAL MEETINGS

Each organizing committee will run its meetings in a different way. If, as an administrator, you are interested in converting an existing school, either public or private, at first you will probably convene meetings of key staff people and evaluate the pros and cons. You, like other charter school organizers, will need to define your mission and, after initial discussions, enlarge your committee to include parent and community representatives. Other organizing committees will, like their proposed schools, be starting "from scratch".

Your early meetings should have three major objectives: to become acquainted with those in your group and with their reasons for wanting to become involved, to get a feel for the feasibility of a charter school and of the work entailed, and to define your school's mission.

The following suggestions for your first four meetings are just that: suggestions. It is necessary to realize from the beginning that, with charter schools, very little is carved in stone. You will become quite adept in being flexible and responding to the needs of your particular situation.

First meeting

The first meeting should be devoted to getting to know the persons attending the meeting and their reasons for being there. Let those present introduce themselves and briefly describe their backgrounds. As you will be dividing up tasks at later meetings, it is important to know the talents and experiences of each member of your group.

The bulk of the meeting can be spent in discussing each person's reasons for wishing to establish a charter school. Some of these reasons will be expressed in positive terms. However, meeting attendees should have ample opportunity to explain why they are dissatisfied with their current situation. Let them have a chance to express the pent-up negative feelings which it may not have been appropriate to express in other groups and which have propelled them to come to this meeting. This first meeting will be a sounding board for the participants' hurt and worries. This will be the first of many bonding experiences as your committee assumes and continues to assume in the days ahead one of its roles—that of a support group.

However, two provisos need to be observed. First, write down each of the comments, positive or negative, on a flip chart. These comments will be a basis for developing positive school objectives and should be kept as a resource for the next meeting and for future referral.

Second, once these negative thoughts have been expressed, all discussions at future meetings should focus on the positive. Undoubtedly, there will be meeting participants who attend only to use the meetings as a personal forum for their complaints. They know that they are among those who are sympathetic to their experiences, but they must not be allowed to dominate the meetings nor to divert attention from the objective of exploring charter school possibilities. As pointed out by Joy Fitzgerald, "Dissatisfaction with the status quo, even if well justified, is not sufficient grounds for a charter" (1995, p. 25).

Don't try to accomplish too much at this meeting. Just let those attending become comfortable with each other in an informal, nonjudgmental environment.

Second meeting

It is of crucial importance, both in creating and then running a successful charter school, that all parties agree on the school's mission. Many problems can be avoided by clearly defining the school's mission in the initial meetings. During the second meeting the goal should be to determine tentative objectives on which there is consensus, as well as areas of disagreement.

Meeting participants should express their individual thoughts as to the charter school's mission: the general type of school they want, curriculum ideas, initial and future grade levels and size, etc. Again, write down all the ideas and encourage brainstorming. Go back to the reasons expressed during the earlier meeting and couch them in positive terms. Some meeting participants may have objectives that are so removed from the general consensus that they will not be interested in further participation. Others may have ideas which initially appear foreign, but will spur discussion and contribute to a better mission statement. Be open to ideas which may challenge or revise your theories. Note the areas of consensus and differences as the starting point for future discussion.

Is there enough consensus and are there enough participants who want to continue to work towards a charter school? Should your charter school idea be pursued (at least by this group)? If enough of those present are interested, set up your third meeting.

Third meeting

Call your state department of education and ask them either to send a speaker or to refer you to a state association of charter schools or a charter school technical support group, which can provide one. For instance, in some states there are charter school networks, e.g., the California Network of Educational Charters (CANEC) and the Colorado League of Charter Schools. Also, ask them to send materials on setting up a charter school as well as a charter school application.

If a lawyer has not already joined your committee, make sure that one is in attendance at this meeting. As you will soon discover, you will need legal advice in a wide range of areas, ranging from the feasibility of your charter school idea to the development of your application and the effects of existing statutes on your school's operations. Look for a lawyer with experience in business and labor law and, if possible, charter school law. It is important that your lawyer not only have expertise, but also be intimately familiar with your school and its mission. If you cannot find a lawyer who is interested in becoming part of your committee, see if you can establish a continuing relationship with one who will work for you on a pro bono basis.

The speaker at this meeting should discuss the history of charter schools in your state; the experiences of charter schools in your school district (especially their relations with the school board); the application procedure; the financial and other support services available for charter schools; the legal requirements which charter schools must meet, both under the charter school law and under other state laws; the pitfalls to avoid; and what it really takes to start a charter school. Ensure plenty of time for questions and discussion so that everyone present is completely clear as to what is required, the odds as to whether the sponsoring agency will accept charter school applications, etc.

Conclude by asking the participants to do soul-searching as to whether they feel the group should pursue the charter school idea and as to whether they individually wish to be involved. Request that they attend the next meeting so that they may share their views even if they do not wish to continue with the group.

Fourth meeting

Begin the meeting with the participants expressing their views on the proposal's prospects. If the group decides to continue, those who no longer wish to participate can then have the opportunity to leave.

At this point it would be wise to revisit the objectives set forth at the second meeting. With this core group of dedicated participants, who have listened to the speaker, reviewed the materials, and done some soul-searching, is there still consensus on some of the earlier objectives and still differences on the others? Now is the time to state your charter school's mission clearly and concisely. Write an initial mission statement which reflects the areas of consensus. A mission statement is a brief, written expression of your school's vision: the goals to be attained and the philosophy and tenets driving the achievement of these goals. It is, in effect, your school's "raison d'être". Make sure that yours is narrowly-focused so that it is defined not only for your committee, but for others who might be interested in the school. As Fitzgerald emphasizes, "Be clear from the outset about the vision of what you want the school to accomplish and the academic standards you hold for students. All key stakeholders should be involved in the process of articulating this vision and [this] should precede any discussion about the technical aspects of the application" (1995, pp. 24, 25).

You can now put a notice in the local newspaper that your committee plans to submit a charter school proposal.

You have taken the first step in your charter school journey.

Stepping Stone 3

....

Maximize Your Organizing Committee's Utilization of the Four E's: Expertise, Efficiency, Effectiveness, and Enterprise

A charter school is both a school and a business. Each of you has chosen to establish a charter school for a different reason or reasons. In almost all cases those reasons are reflected in your initial mission statement and relate to your providing a particular educational program. Even if your reasons are not related to an educational program, it is unlikely that you have chosen the charter school route because you want to open your own business. Yet, that is exactly what you will be doing.

So far you have concentrated on your mission statement. You expect to flesh out this statement so that you can come up with the curriculum, parent involvement strategies, student recruitment plans, etc. that will be needed to effectuate your mission. However, there will be many other issues such as budget, governance structure, and employment policy which you will also have to resolve during the application process. In doing so, you will need to visualize your school as a business.

Preparing a charter school application is a complicated process. The trail to your charter school now becomes steeper. This is a good time to develop the organizational attributes which will facilitate the administration of your business: your school. They may be grouped under the Four E's: expertise, efficiency, effectiveness, and enterprise.

EXPERTISE

You have formed a core group of school organizers and enlisted the services of a lawyer, either as a committee member or on a pro bono basis. Now is the time either to add to your committee or to make arrangements with those persons who have the types of expertise which you will need. The *Colorado Charter School Information Packet and Handbook* advises, "Seek out people who have skills in finance, facilities, curriculum and instruction, management practices, and school law, to name a few" (Windler, 1997, p. 12).

Foremost among these will be an accountant. Try to find one who is adept in financial analysis and who has experience in both bookkeeping and school finance.

Recruit one or two businessmen from the community. The CEO of a business or a banker would be especially helpful. Likewise, someone from a social services organization or a minister would be able to provide insights on recruiting and providing services to at-risk students and their families. Persons familiar with special education and assessment techniques will give you a leg up in these often challenging areas. If you need to find a site, you will also need to work closely with a realtor, a building inspector, and perhaps an architect.

In each case try to recruit these "experts" as organizing committee or subcommittee members. This failing, work on securing their services on a continuing pro bono basis. Nearby colleges and universities may be good sources for providing the specialized services you will need.

Committee members can develop their own expertise. Check first with your state department of education and your sponsoring agency. Some departments are founts of information, providing detailed handbooks on creating a charter school, furnishing lists of existing charter schools, holding workshops, and answering questions. At the very least, they should provide to you or direct you to copies of your state's charter school law, school finance law, school law book, and code of regulations. Your sponsoring agency should be able to provide you with information on its deadlines and specific application procedures.

Check Appendix C to see whether there is an association of charter schools in your state which will provide assistance and networking opportunities and/or an organization which can provide technical support. Abby R. Weiss has stressed the need for this outside assistance, both in providing "the eyes of an outsider" and the backing of a charter school "community" (1997, pp. 21-22).

Benefit from the expertise of those who have established successful charter schools. Contact or visit charter schools, especially those with a similar educational program or those chartered by your sponsoring agency. It may even be worthwhile for you to send a committee member to visit an out-of-state school or to attend a large charter school conference.

The number of web sites providing information is rapidly increasing. In April 1997 the U.S. Department of Education in cooperation with WestEd and the California State University Institute for Education Reform set up a national web site, which not only enables you to search other charter school sites on the Internet, but also provides information files, a resource directory and links, and access to information on specific charter schools (U.S. Department of Education, WestEd, and California State University Institute for Education Reform).

In addition to learning about charter schools, you would be well advised to check out research on what makes an effective school. Two of the books which may prove helpful are *How to Make a Better School,* which covers curriculum development and evaluation, extracurricular activities, teaching strategies, student assessment, and the hiring, evaluation, and supervision of teachers (McQuade and Champagne, 1995); and *Politics, Markets, and America's Schools,* which points to the common strands in administrative leadership, teaching personnel, and programs found in successful schools (Chubb and Moe, 1990).

If you need further assistance, Appendix C will guide you to other sources of information.

EFFICIENCY

Now is the time to introduce some structure into your organizing committee and its proceedings. A good place to begin is the selection of officers and the division of responsibilities.

Officers

A chairperson, a vice chairperson, and a secretary are customary organizing committee officers. The duties of each should extend beyond those involved in the chairing of meetings, the taking of minutes, and the handling of correspondence, important as these will be.

Subcommittees

Your organizing committee members will undoubtedly be involved with multiple tasks and may serve on more than one subcommittee. These subcommittees should also include persons with expertise who are not part of your organizing committee. Determine whether your subcommittees will cover narrow or broad areas. Look at the checklist of organizational plan elements (Table 5 page 50) and add to it such items as networking, marketing, and research. For which of these areas do you want to have a separate subcommittee and which areas do you want to combine? If you decide to establish fewer subcommittees, you might want to adopt some of the broader subheadings used in Stepping Stone 4:

• educational program,
• students and student services,
• other school constituencies,
• site and site support,
• administration,
• legal issues, and
• budget.

The subcommittees you establish may also depend on whether you will be a conversion or a "from-scratch" school. Be aware, however, that those schools converting to charter status will be making a number of changes in their programs as well as assuming the additional tasks involved in running their own schools. The size of your school may also impact your subcommittee structure.

How often will your subcommittees report to the committee as a whole? If you have a number of narrowly focused subcommittees, you might wish to stagger their reports so that those whose work can be accomplished more quickly will report their results earlier. If there are fewer subcommittees, you may want each to report on its progress at each meeting and establish target dates for the final reports. In either case, such subcommittees as site selection will probably need to report to the whole committee at each meeting, and all committees should be encouraged to present pressing issues and questions at any meeting.

Budget

Some of the organizing committee's responsibilities might be assigned to the committee as a whole as opposed to a subcommittee. Especially consider adopting this approach with your budget.

Your budget will be the tangible expression of your school's mission. The ways in which you spend your money will reflect the priorities of your school and should demand the whole committee's consideration and consensus. As each subcommittee submits its progress and final reports, the costs of the alternatives presented can be fed into your emerging budget document. Through this document, the committee can better determine how to prioritize expenditure options within the limits of expected revenues. It will also be aware of any increases in revenues resulting from your fund-raising efforts.

The accountant on your committee should be responsible for keeping the budget and determining the financial implications of various spending options.

Master calendar

A master calendar will be an important part of your planning process. Include subcommittee reporting dates, sponsoring agency deadlines, and target dates for completing specific tasks such as your demographic profile and job descriptions. Like the budget, the calendar will be a work in progress and will be invaluable both before and after your school's start-up. Assign someone on your committee to be in charge of the calendar.

Other responsibilities

If you are in a state that does not allow blanket waivers from certain state and local laws and regulations, it may be a good idea to have someone keep a running record of the waivers which you might wish to secure. Consider setting up a timeline showing the periods during which various tasks should be performed. Make sure that agendas are prepared for committee and subcommittee meetings and that minutes are taken.

EFFECTIVENESS

Expertise and efficiency increase the effectiveness of your charter school development process. Likewise, drafting a comprehensive organizational plan, as described in Stepping Stone 4, should contribute both to the approval of your charter and your school's subsequent start-up and operation. Addressing the two factors discussed below should also increase the effectiveness of your efforts.

Political issues

"Do not underestimate the extent to which this is a political process." So stated Fitzgerald in her Colorado charter school study (1995, p. 25). Charter school developers should be cognizant of the political factors which will impact the approval of their charter school.

Describing some of the opposition which charter schools may face, the Little Hoover Commission's report stated:

> Some fear that charter schools will become isolated, elite campuses of excellence that will doom the large numbers of children left out to mediocre educations. Others worry that charter schools are a backdoor way of subsidizing religious teachings with public dollars. Some unions believe that employees' rights will not be adequately protected and that hard-won benefits will disap-

pear. Education administrators, deeply engrained with
the habit of procedural accountability, believe that
relaxed or non-existent rules are an invitation to corrup-
tion, graft and scandal. School districts are often uncom-
fortable with the unaccustomed role of outcome
oversight (1996, p. 12).

The National Education Association listed among the
questions that community leaders might ask: "How will the
charter school program attract businesses and professionals
to the community? Will our taxes be affected? How well prepared will the students be to move to higher education? To
employment after high school?" (1995, p. 16).

In Urahn and Stewart's survey of concerns expressed by
Minnesota school board members in their debates on charter
school proposals, their two foremost concerns were the effect
on the district (primarily the loss of revenue and the draining
of resources) and philosophical issues (especially lack of support and accountability) (1994, pp. 24-31).

Charter school developers need to do the homework
necessary to determine the potential issues and then formulate strategies for meeting them when or, preferably,
before they are raised.

Doing research to gain expertise on the overall charter
school movement and on particular issues is a crucial com-
ponent of preparing for criticism. Another strategy is to
enlist allies.

Start out by making your community aware of your
plans. Develop a close relationship with the media and issue
periodic reports on your progress. Get out into the community and speak before as many community groups as you can.
Hold public meetings at which you will present your plans

and answer questions. These meetings should be focused on securing community support.

Target specific organizations. One way of doing this is establishing a relationship with a college or university. Other charter schools have ties to community organizations and even city governments. In addition to the know-how and financial benefits which such an alliance can provide, you will have greater credibility.

Your credibility can be further enhanced by the community and business leaders who become your allies (Fitzgerald, 1995, p. 25). Make sure that your mayor, city council, state senator, and state representative are informed of your proposal and of its support in the community. Consider inviting these leaders to your meetings and seek their input.

You will need to target those groups whose support is essential to your charter's approval. In California charter school petitions must be signed by 50 percent of the teachers in a school or 10 percent of the teachers in a school district (Vergari and Mintrom, 1996. p. 21). Develop strategies for persuading these teachers to sign. In New Hampshire voters must authorize the existence of charter schools within their school district before proposals can be considered (p. 47). In this case you will be seeking the support of a wide range of voter constituencies.

Also, perhaps surprisingly, it makes sense to establish relationships with those who may be opposed to your school. Those with objections may be your school's potential neighbors, the teacher union, school district staff, a newspaper editor, or even some of the teachers at your current school who regard your proposal as a criticism of their teaching methods. Get in touch with key individuals, invite them to a meeting, find out their concerns, and address their issues.

Of special importance is getting to know each member of your sponsoring agency board. Determine whether he or she is opposed to charter schools in general and, if so, why. What issues are important to each of them? The feedback they provide and the personal relationships you develop may be what tilts the scales when their vote is cast.

Time element

You will have secured from your sponsoring agency the deadlines you must meet during your application process. How much time does meeting the next application deadline give you? How much time would you have between approval and getting your school into operation by the beginning of the school year? If you were to go through an appeals process, by how much would that preoperational period be shortened?

In Medler and Nathan's survey of 110 charter schools, school representatives were asked what advice they would give to charter school developers. Ranked second, behind only the establishment of and commitment to a clear mission, was "Give yourself plenty of time to plan" (1995, p. 30). This advice was echoed by Dr. Sam Pantleo, administrator of the Pueblo School for the Arts and Sciences in Pueblo, Colorado, who advised, "Start planning a year in advance" (Interview, 1997).

Likewise, a survey of 225 charter schools conducted as part of the National Study of Charter Schools showed that "lack of planning time" was the second greatest barrier to these schools' development and implementation (RPP International and University of Minnesota, 1997, p. 35).

In brief, avoid going in with a half-baked proposal. Leave enough time to develop an application that will be approved and that will facilitate opening your school within what may be a tight time frame. Include on your organizing committee some parents whose children will be in the lower grades of your school so that if you need to wait a year or two, they will still be interested. The important outcome is the creation of your charter school, not the year in which it is created.

Finally, you should take time to think about Plan B, the course of action you will take if your first efforts to navigate the charter approval process do not succeed. Plan B is discussed in Stepping Stone 5.

ENTERPRISE

....

Merriam Webster's Collegiate Dictionary defines enterprise as "readiness to engage in daring action" (1996, p. 386). Enterprise is the spirit which will drive your committee, enabling it to seek innovative solutions, to meet each new challenge.

As noted charter school administrator Yvonne Chan so enthusiastically proclaimed in her keynote address at the fourth annual California charter school conference, "And if there's no answer out there, then for heaven's sake, make up your own answer" (1997).

Stepping Stone 4

....

Develop a Detailed Plan for Your School's Operation and Incorporate All or Part of It into Your Application

"View the charter application as a planning tool rather than a 'hurdle' on the way to obtaining a charter." So recommended a group of charter school experts at a September 1995 workshop in Seattle (Millot and Lake, 1996, p. 35). Indeed, your application should be not just a planning tool, but a detailed plan for your school's operation.

YOUR SCHOOL'S PLAN
....

You have already secured information on your state's application requirements. These may be spelled out in an application form or in a list of elements which your application must include.

Table 4 shows the charter application elements required in three states: California, Colorado, and Massachusetts. Educational program, employment policy, enrollment policy, governance, learning objectives, and student assessment must be addressed in all three states. However, there are many elements which are required in only one or two of the states' applications. Further, areas such as food services, purchasing procedures, custodial services, maintenance, groundskeeping, bookkeeping, a library, a computer laboratory, public relations, and school expansion are not men-

Table 4   Specifically Required Application Contents

Element	Calif.	Colo.	Mass.
Annual audit	x	x	
Budget		x	x
Day in life of student			x
Displacement plan	x	x	
District dispute procedures	x		
Economically sound/fund-raising		x	
Educational program	x	x	x
Employment policy	x	x	x
Employee evaluation			x
Employee qualifications	x		x
Professional development			x
Retirement coverage	x		
Rights in former district	x		
Enrollment policy	x	x	x
Recruiting/marketing			x
Reflective racial/ethnic balance	x		
Evidence of support		x	x
Founding coalition profile			x
Governance	x	x	x
Health/safety	x		
Innovation		x	x
Learning objectives	x	x	x
Legal liability/insurance		x	
Mission statement		x	x
Need for school			x
Parent/community involvement	x	x	
Pupil behavior/suspension-expulsion	x		x
School accountability		x	
School demographics	x		x
Site			x
Special education services			x
Student assessment	x	x	x
Timetable			x
Transportation		x	x

Source: "CANEC's Characteristics of Strong Charter Petitions", 1997, pp. 1, 4; Little Hoover Commission, 1996, p. 112; Commonwealth of Massachusetts, Department of Education, 1997a, pp. 11-15; Commonwealth of Massachusetts, Department of Education, 1997c, p. 2; Windler, 1997, Appendix A, pp. 3-4.

tioned in any of these states' requirements. Yet, each will warrant consideration in planning your school's operation.

In preparing your application, visualize what will be needed for your school's actual operation and formulate an organizational plan which will cover all of these areas. Check with your sponsoring agency to determine the succinctness or detail which it prefers in its applications and look at other successful applications. If you are to fill out an application form, complete the required areas. Determine from your sponsoring agency what supplemental information may be added. Also, consider whether including too much detail in your charter application will inhibit the flexibility of your design and program (Premack, 1997b, p. 9). Regardless of whether all or part of your organizational plan will be submitted in your application, draw up a comprehensive plan,

Table 5 provides a checklist of the elements which you may need to include in your organizational plan. You should address all those issues which you anticipate your school will face. (You will be elaborating upon and refining this plan when you draw up a management plan during the preoperational period between application approval and school start-up.)

Looking at the early experiences of Minnesota's charter schools, Sue Urahn and Dan Stewart concluded, "The four areas in which charter schools are experiencing the greatest difficulty are transportation, facilities, special education, and their relationship with the sponsoring district" (1994, p. 46). On the other hand, when schools in Medler and Nathan's 1995 charter school survey were asked to rank nine barriers to establishing and operating their schools, those ranked as most difficult to overcome were lack of start-up funds, finances, facilities, and internal process/conflict (1995, p.

Table 5	Checklist of Organizational Plan Elements

❏ Administration
❏ Audit
❏ Behavior code
❏ Bookkeeping
❏ Budgets
❏ Community involvement
❏ Computer laboratory
❏ Curriculum/instructional approach
❏ Custodial services/maintenance
❏ Demographic profile
❏ Displacement plan
❏ District relations
❏ Economic viability
❏ Employment policy
❏ Enrollment policy
❏ Evidence of support
❏ Expansion plans
❏ Food services
❏ Founding coalition profile
❏ Fund-raising
❏ Governance
❏ Groundskeeping

❏ Health/safety
❏ Innovation
❏ Insurance/liability
❏ Legal status
❏ Library
❏ Mission statement
❏ Need for school
❏ Outcomes
❏ Parent involvement
❏ Payroll
❏ Public relations
❏ Purchasing procedures
❏ School accountability
❏ School demographics
❏ Security
❏ Site
❏ Special education
❏ Student assessment
❏ Student recruitment
❏ Timetable
❏ Transportation
❏ Warehousing

28). You cannot foresee which elements are the most important to your application or which issues might cause your
school the most problems. If your organizational plan is a
complete one, you will have covered all the bases.

This is important for four reasons. First, it will assure that
your application is complete in meeting your state's requirements. Second, it will show your sponsoring agency's review-
ers that you have done your homework, that you have
anticipated their questions, and that you have planned for
various eventualities. A number of charter school applications have been turned down because they were sketchy,
incomplete, and/or unrealistic. The lack of planning reflected
in these applications did not offer much promise that the
schools' organizers would be capable of operating successful
charter schools.

Third, you may have a very short period between your
charter's approval and your start-up date. Having an organizational plan in hand will greatly expedite your efforts to
make your school operational.

Finally, and of utmost importance, your organizational
plan will be invaluable in your school's operation:

- The clarity of your mission statement will aid you in
  attracting the parents and staff who are in accord with
  your philosophy.
- You will have assessment tools through which not only
  your school, but also parents, your sponsoring agency,
  and your community can measure student progress.
- You will have written a description of your school's program and policies that will serve you as a continuing
  point of reference and will facilitate your fund-raising
  efforts.
- You will have minimized conflict by carefully establishing
  criteria for the selection of your administrator and your

governing board and by delineating their responsibilities.
• You will have set your priorities through your school's budget and will have planned for its fiscal viability.

The charter school which you establish will be unique. Its location, its mission, the people involved, its day-to-day operations will be distinct to your school. As you examine the organizational areas which you must consider and as you arrive at decisions in each area, remember that the right answers are those which are best for your particular situation, for your particular school. The discussions in this stepping stone of the individual issues which charter schools must address are intended to provide useful information and insights which will help you reach your own answers.

BALANCING SCHOOL DISTRICT SERVICES AND YOUR SCHOOL'S AUTONOMY

You will discover that one continuing issue runs through the organizational areas: the extent to which you should utilize the services of your school district. Joe Schneider and Marcella Dianda have noted, "Central-office staff have one thing the charter school wants: expertise in legal, accounting, purchasing, and liability matters" (1995, p. 22). Eric Premack pointed out that the services which a school district might provide "include transportation, food services, facilities maintenance and operations, groundskeeping, custodial, security, fiscal management, personnel, curriculum development, assessment and testing, purchasing and warehousing, and legal counsel" (1997a, p. 50).

You will want to achieve a balance between the ease of relying on district services, the expertise which the districts can provide, and the advantages of size which they offer (e.g., in insurance coverage, bookkeeping systems) versus autonomy, with all that it implies for innovation and site-based control, whether in curriculum, priority setting, or funding arrangements. If your charter school is to reject the lessons of those who have preceded you, will you be reinventing the wheel? If your charter school is to rely entirely upon district services, what is your rationale for becoming a charter school? You must determine the balance which is best for you. Financial considerations will impact this balance. They will stem in large part from whether it will be more economical for you to use the district's services (if it agrees to supply them), provide them yourself, contract with others (if this is permitted in your state), or utilize some other financial option. However, it also will be affected by your state's procedures for financing charter schools, i.e., the way in which you can arrange for or opt out of your school district's provision of specific services.

For instance, in Colorado you will negotiate for a percentage of your school district's per pupil operating revenue and then contract with the school district if you wish it to provide particular services.

In California, you have several options:

- If you are a conversion school, you may choose to continue to receive the same resources and per-pupil funding allocation which you received as a regular public school. Will you then be contributing to district services you do not want or need and will you be restricting yourself from adopting cost-saving alternatives? Can you/will you opt out of a service and reallocate the funding to other services (BW Associates, 1994a, pp. 5–6; Premack, 1997a, pp. 31–34)?

- You might instead choose to receive revenues from your school district for all the categorical programs to which you are entitled to receive funding. Be aware that you will need to undertake the often difficult task of determining which program funds might be available and for which ones you have eligibility, that districts often do not know the per school cost of programs, and that districts may be covering high-cost programs, such as special education, by supplementing federal and state funding with money from their general funds (Premack, 1997a, pp. 7, 11).

• Perhaps you will just choose, with your California district's agreement, to have it "pass through" to you your full state entitlement (BW Associates, 1994a, p. 5).

• Perhaps California's pilot program of direct state funding (bypassing school districts) will have become a statewide option (Patterson, 1997, p. 6).

• Perhaps, you will reach a negotiated agreement with your school district (BW Associates, 1994a, p. 6).

These are just examples of the financial intricacies which you may face. In making your decisions, you will need to be intimately familiar with all the ins and outs of your particular state's funding provisos.

You must also assess for each area of your organizational plan the pros and cons of various provider options. It is now time to examine the organizational areas.

EDUCATIONAL PROGRAM

Your school's mission statement, its grade levels and size, its outcomes, its curriculum/instructional approach, and its student assessment are integral, interrelated parts of your overall educational program.

Mission

Of primary importance is your mission statement. A report by BW Associates stated, "In schools that have thought through their educational vision, it is clear that the decisions they have made are all derived from their vision. . . . For new schools starting up as charters, this step is particularly critical since the struggles with launching a new enterprise may prove daunting, but a clear vision will help the developers stay focused" (1994b, pp. 3-4). Ginny Jaramillo, administrator of Park County, Colorado's Lake George-Guffey Charter School, offered as her one piece of advice to charter school developers: "[Operate] from a very clear, strong vision", not just to get approved, but "just to survive and succeed" (Interview, 1996).

Must you have an innovative mission? Check for requirements in your state. What exactly is innovative? Finn, Manno, and Bierlein have pointed out, "Where progressivism reigns as local orthodoxy, a back-to-basics school signifies innovation—and vice-versa" (1996, p. 21).

Whether or not a school's mission is innovative also depends on your sponsoring agency. In Massachusetts the state board of education, the sponsoring agency, seeks charter schools which do not duplicate earlier state models (Pioneer Institute for Public Policy Research, 1996, p. VIII-8). In contrast, in Colorado, where school districts sponsor charter schools, in 1997 Montessori school proposals were approved in two neighboring counties, Douglas and Jefferson. Each was unique in its own school district, if not in the state.

You have been working on your mission statement since your early organizational meetings. Continue to reexamine it as you develop your charter school application.

Grade levels, size, and target population

Each application must include a statement of the school's grade levels, its projected enrollment, and, if applicable, its target population. This statement may be presented on a fact sheet prefacing your application or included in your mission statement, your goals, or some other part of your application. It provides the most basic information about your school and should be developed in concurrence with your mission.

You may choose to start with your entire grade range or, on the other hand, might begin with a limited number of grades and then expand, adding a grade each year. If you plan to expand, get your charter for the projected grade range so that you do not have to go back later and apply for another charter.

Examine the grade levels you will serve in terms of the public school system's school structure. Denver's Clayton Charter School, which started out as a kindergarten, was designed to serve children throughout their early childhood (preschool through grade three). Expanding to cover that period, first as a private school and then as a charter school, it discovered that parents were reluctant to switch their children into a school for just one year and then have to make the transition into a different elementary school for the two years preceding middle school. Clayton had no third grade waiting list (Bingham, 1997).

Should you start large or start small? At the Franklin, Massachusetts charter school conference Patricia Karl of the Lawrence Family Development Charter School explained how her school had increased its initial size to 180 students after being advised that a larger school would be more economical (Pioneer Institute..., 1996, p. viii-9). On the other hand, as a "from-scratch" school you may wish to follow the example of such charter schools as Colorado's Pueblo School for the Arts and Sciences and The EXCEL School in Durango, each of which gained operational experience as a charter school before expanding. A charter school usually draws students from families in their neighborhood, from families who believe in the school's mission, and/or from families who view the school as a preferable alternative to their child's current school. If your target population is children who are at-risk or require special education services, be aware that you will need to provide extra support services and cover the costs which they entail. These services may be extra personnel, such as a counselor or reading specialist, or family support services. One school, Colorado Springs' Community Prep School, has established a voucher support system. The school has set up accounts with doctors, dentists, child care providers, gas stations, etc., so that its at-risk students can pay for needed services with vouchers (Interview with Rodriguez, 1997).

Outcomes

In developing your application, your outcomes (learning objectives) will arise from the goals articulated in your mission statement. Your curriculum and instructional approach will be chosen or designed to achieve these outcomes, and your assessment tools will measure the extent to which these outcomes have been reached (BW Associates, 1994b, p. 5). Generally, your curriculum and assessment decisions will be made after you have determined your outcomes, but, if, for instance, you already know that you wish to have a Montessori curriculum, you will be choosing the curriculum first and then the outcomes which that curriculum promotes.

What kind of outcomes do you want? The outcomes should be clear and measurable. If not, it will be difficult to choose the curriculum best suited to your purpose and almost impossible to choose assessment tools that can determine whether they have been achieved. Outcomes should address content and process, knowledge and performance. They should be meaningful to the students and to their lives as adults (BW Associates, 1994b, p. 6).

Secure a copy of your state or school district standards. Choose either to adopt these standards (you may be required to do so) or develop your own. In the latter case, document how your school will meet or exceed the required standards (Windler, 1997, p. 6).

In developing your own outcomes, look at those which have been used in school districts, state boards of education, private schools, and other charter schools and adapt them to your specific situation. You will soon learn how to write concise, meaningful, measurable outcomes.

Outcomes should be determined through the consensus of those on your organizing committee. Even though you will probably have one of your committees doing the groundwork in this area, it should be responsive to the input and views of the whole committee.

BW Associates suggested a procedure for developing outcomes, whereby first "five to ten significant exit outcomes that emphasize useful knowledge and complex performances" are determined and then "schools should 'design down' from exit outcomes to create meaningful curricula with course and program outcomes that serve as signposts of progress" (BW Associates, 1994c, p. 3). In other words, once you have decided the major outcomes which you want your students to have achieved by the time they leave your school, determine, for each grade level and domain, the outcomes that students should fulfill to progress to those final outcomes. You will also want to break down each goal into specific objectives. This can be done during the school's preoperational period and reassessed and revised during the school's operation.

Curriculum/instructional approach

One feature of the charter school movement is the variety in their curricula and approaches. Table 6 lists a number of the curricula and instructional approaches which have been used by charter schools.

Other curricula/instructional approaches may meet your needs. For instance, the New American Schools coalition includes seven different educational designs: ATLAS Communities, The Audrey Cohen College System of Education, Co-NECT Schools, Expeditionary Learning Outward Bound, Modern Red Schoolhouse, National Alliance for Restructuring Education, and Roots and Wings (Education Commission of the States, 1996).

If you choose an established curriculum, study it carefully as you will want to adapt it to your student population. Also, determine if it will fulfill all your program's requirements.

If you live in a state which permits privatization, you may decide to go a step further and have a for-profit company, such as Alternative Public Schools; the Edison Project, LLC; Kids 1, Inc.; or Sabis Educational Systems, Inc. operate your school and implement its curriculum.

The Glossary briefly describes some of the established curricula you might use; addresses from which you may secure further information are included in the Resources appendix.

If you choose to develop your own curriculum, you will need to devote a considerable amount of time to the task. Contact and visit other schools using a similar approach and

Table 6 Charter School Curricula and Instructional Approaches

Accelerated Schools Model
American Sign Language
Basic Skills
CATO
Character Development
Coalition of Essential Schools
College Preparatory
Community Service Projects
Computer-Driven
Cooperative Learning
Core Knowledge Sequence
Direct Instruction
Distance Learning
Dual Language
Edison Project
Efficacy
Experiential Learning
High/Scope
Home-Based Study
Independent Study
Individually-Based Instruction
Integrated Curriculum
Integrated Thematic Instruction
International Baccalaureate
International Issues
Junior Great Books
Montessori
Multiple Intelligences
Paideia
Reggio Emilia
SABIS
School-to-Work
Seminars
Technology-Intensive
Tutorials
Urban Learning Community
Visual and Performing Arts
Vocational
Waldorf Education
Work Experience

Source: Dale, 1996, pp. 1-66; "A Profile of California's Charter Schools....". 1996, pp. 2-89.

utilize their guidelines and insights. Specify how the curriculum will achieve your outcomes and grade and subject objectives. Since there is no written curriculum guide, you will need to ensure that all your school's stakeholders both understand and are in accord with your curriculum.

The curriculum you choose will be an important determinant of your classroom structure and schedule. For instance, should your classes be set up by grade or in multiage groupings? Which groupings make the most sense in terms of your curriculum, the children's developmental ages, and your enrollment? Likewise, your curriculum and classroom structure (and budget) will affect your staffing needs. Will you have one teacher per classroom, a teacher plus a teacher's assistant, teaching teams, student interns, and/or volunteers?

Colorado's Lake George-Guffey Charter School has two locations. In its first year of operation (1996–97) both locations used multi-age groupings with single teachers. Guffey, with an enrollment of 34, had groups K–3 and 3–6. Lake George, with an enrollment of 136, had groups P (3, 4 and 5 year olds), K–1, 1–2, 2–3, 4–5, 5–6, and 6–7. Jaramillo indicated that during the next year team teaching (with two teachers) might be introduced at Lake George with 1–3 and 3–5 classrooms (Interview, 1996). Play around with which classroom structure will best suit your educational program.

Do you want to follow your district's calendar? Gifford and Keller's survey of 120 Arizona charter school teachers revealed that 62% of their schools operated for nine months, 22% for ten months, and 16% year round. While 58% followed the traditional daily schedule, 26% had morning and afternoon sessions and 15% offered a three-session day (morning, afternoon, evening) (1996, pp. 3-4). Referring to the three session day, Gifford and Keller pointed out, "Such innovative schedules allow students, especially at-risk students, to attend classes that best fit their individual needs. These schedules also give students the opportunity to participate in mentoring programs, internships, and work a part-time job" (pp. 3-4).

Choose the schedule which best suits your educational program within the constraints imposed by the costs of additional hours, the availability of your site (if you share it with other users), the extracurricular activities you will offer, and transportation options. With respect to the last constraint, Urahn and Stewart in their Minnesota charter school report, observed, "The charter schools are frustrated because they must coordinate their calendars and starting times in order to fit the district's transportation schedule. This makes it difficult to structure anything but a traditional schedule" (1994, p. 46).

Also, bear in mind that you must fulfill (or seek a waiver or variance from) any state/district requirements for a minimum number of hours of teacher-pupil contact and/or teacher-pupil instruction. Can "lunch, recess, passing time, study halls, before and after school programs" be included ("Educational Process Defined", 1994, pp. 1-2)? Will it make a difference if teachers are eating with the children or interacting with them on the playground?

It is imperative that your school receive its full funding allocation. This may pose a problem if your school, like a number of charter schools, follows a unique schedule. For instance, as a report of the Wisconsin Association of School Boards described the Minnesota New Country School in LeSueur: "The school has no classes, no attendance requirements and no grades. Instead, students work through a curriculum guide on projects leading to demonstrated competencies in nine general areas. . . . During the school day, most are out in the community doing projects, working as interns or participating in community service and post-secondary options activities . . ." (1996, p. 8).

If your state uses a pupil count day to determine school enrollment, you will need to make a special effort to assure students' attendance on that day and to discover whether off-site attendance qualifies. If funds are allocated on the basis of ADA (average daily attendance) and there is a minimum number of days per school year, you not only may need to determine what qualifies as attendance, but also be forced either to rearrange your scheduling or to secure a waiver so that you will not lose your full apportionment credit (Premack, 1997a, p. 42).

Student assessment

There is a great variety in the assessment tools which charter schools use, with schools often using more than one assessment tool.

Assessment tools fall within three types: norm-referenced (or standardized) tests in which a student's scores are compared with those of the sample group used to determine typical performance; criterion-referenced tests in which a student's scores measure the extent to which his/her performance meets established performance standards; and performance assessment, an assessment that occurs as a student functions in his/her school environment.

Charter schools can evaluate the already-available norm-referenced and criterion-referenced tests to determine which best meet their needs. Some of the types of performance assessment are portfolios, presentations, exhibits, science projects, journals, teacher observation, books read, and research projects. You may wish to enlist the services of someone familiar with student evaluation or of a college or university to help you design your assessment system. Your state or your school district may require the administration of a specified standardized test. If your school finds this test an unsatisfactory measure of your students' progress, try to secure a waiver. If unsuccessful, take time to make sure that your students are familiar with taking tests and test-taking procedures. You may also wish to write a disclaimer of the test's validity for your school that can accompany release of your test scores.

Two principles should guide your selection of assessment tools. First, in order to assure a holistic view of your students' development, choose the tool or tools which measure student progress in a range of domains. Secondly, make sure that your assessment tools provide accurate measurement of the progress students are making in achieving each of the specific outcomes and objectives you have selected for your school. As a BW Associates report emphasized, "The success of charter schools will be judged largely on whether their students achieve the outcomes specified in their charters" (1994b, p. 4).

Your state department of education may have requirements for public schools (including charter schools) on the reporting of student achievement to students, parents, staff, the community, the school board, and the department of education. If not, specify in your organizational plan how you will report your school's performance.

STUDENTS AND STUDENT SERVICES

It should go without saying that your students and the services provided to them belong at the crux of your organizational plan. Apart from your educational program, there are other important areas to address.

Demographic profile

Which students and families will you be serving? Do some research and come up with a demographic profile of the students you expect to attract and/or the geographical area that you will serve. This will be of value in drawing up your organizational plan, in marketing your school to the community and prospective parents, and in serving students and their families.

Develop a profile which includes a determination of the changes occurring in your neighborhood:

- Is it becoming more commercial?
- Is the population aging or have more young families moved in?
- Has the ethnic mix changed?
- If you are a conversion school, what children will be replacing those children who do not wish to continue at your school when it becomes a charter school and will they have different needs?

You may be setting up your school specifically to serve high-risk children, drop-outs, or those with a hearing disability. You will still need to seek the answers to such questions as to how large your recruitment area will be and whether there will be a number of ESL (English as a second language) children.

Regardless of your school's mission, try to determine:

- the number of two- or single-parent households;
- household income level;
- single-family houses, apartments, and public housing units;
- parent educational levels;
- working or stay-at-home mothers;
- parents unemployed or working two or more jobs;
- the crime rate;

- the public transportation system;
- and the community facilities which can be used in your recruitment efforts and as a resource for your school's program.

If you take time now to get to know your area, you will be better attuned to your family/student population and better prepared to serve them.

Enrollment policy

Before determining your enrollment policy, check with your sponsoring agency as to any specific requirements. Be aware that you must be nondiscriminatory in your enrollment and may, as in California, need to enroll a student population that reflects the racial/ethnic mix of your area. Understand that nondiscrimination includes acceptance of students with IEP's. If, for instance, your school will have a Montessori program and wishes to accept primarily those children who have attended a Montessori school, determine whether this more restrictive policy will meet nondiscriminatory enrollment requirements.

How will you select students? Here again, check on the regulations. Will preference be given to children already attending or in the attendance area of your conversion school? If you are to be a conversion school, most of your current students will probably continue to attend. For instance, at Roosevelt-Edison Charter School in Colorado Springs, Colorado, 98 percent of the neighborhood children enrolled (Scanlon, 1996a).

There are a number of other questions to consider:
- If a from-scratch school, will priority be given to your own children? If not, what incentive is there for those of

you who are parents to spend countless hours and days setting up the school?

• Will you use a waiting list?
• Will there be a lottery? If so, will the lottery be weighted to assure a gender mix, a racial/ethnic mix, or a mix of children at-risk and not-at-risk?
• Will students be enrolled who live outside of your school district? If so, will preference be given to those within the district?
• Will you give preference to siblings?

These issues must be resolved before you can begin to recruit students.

Recruitment

Your demographic survey should assist you in recruiting students. You may also want to do a survey of families in the community to determine their interest in your school and to develop a database of potential students.

In framing your recruitment policy recall the strategies you pursued in locating your organizing committee members: networking, word-of-mouth, newspaper notices, and the placing of flyers in locations frequented by families. All of these strategies can also be utilized in marketing your school to prospective families. Widespread publicity for your school (including the presentation of information in different languages) is essential not only for your marketing, but also as a means of enrolling a diverse student population.

The Goldwater Institute's survey of 1,600 Arizona charter school parents revealed that 48.4% learned about charter schools from friends, 12.8% from the newspaper, 10% from the community, 1.5% from TV/radio, and 20% from other sources (Gifford, 1996, p. 5). It may be that even though newspapers and TV/radio ranked relatively low, it was from these sources that the friends of charter school parents received their information and then passed it on.

By the time your application is approved, you will have more fully developed your educational program and organizational plan and will be well prepared to present information and answer questions. Schedule meetings in convenient locations and at convenient times to present your school's program to prospective families.

If you are a school for at-risk students, you will also need to clarify the difference between special education students, who have an identified disability, and at-risk students, who are less likely to succeed in a typical school environment because of such factors as being of an ethnic minority or coming from a low-income family. Parents understandably may be reluctant to have their children labeled "at-risk". Possible approaches in this situation are stressing the wide range of services the school will provide and emphasizing that you will be challenging the children to realize their highest potentials.

Additional strategies are placing advertisements in newspapers (hopefully at discounted rates); meeting with real estate agents, local advocacy groups, religious leaders, social workers, probation officers, etc.; and placing flyers in such places as "convenience stores, gas stations, drugstores, fast-food franchises, grocery stores, barbershops, and hairdressers" (Nathan, 1996, pp. 138–140).

Use your own imagination and come up with the recruitment plan which you will be following in the preoperational period.

Finally, for those of you who are with an existing school, don't forget to develop a plan to provide attendance alternatives for those families who decide not to remain at your school once it converts to charter status.

Behavior code

Whether or not your state requires it, you should come up with a general behavior code. This code should be congruent with the philosophy which you are incorporating into your educational plan.

Determine whether your suspension-expulsion policy needs to be the same as that established for your school district and, if necessary, seek a waiver.

You will be elaborating on your behavioral code during your school's preoperational and operational periods. However, you must now make it explicit enough that prospective parents and students will know both your expectations for pupil behavior and the consequences of not meeting them.

Special education

The education of children with identified disabilities will entail the provision of additional services, will incur additional costs, will impose additional challenges to your teaching staff, and will require your familiarity and compliance with an intricate network of federal and state regulations. Referring to Minnesota charter schools, Urahn and Stewart pointed out, "Charter schools face two problems in terms of special education: many were unfamiliar with the special education funding process, and they were unprepared to provide the assessments and services needed" (1994, p. 48). Premack has stressed the need for early attention to this area (1997a, p. 18).

Before making any decisions, you will need to know what is required. Become familiar with the regulations, speak with persons responsible for special education in your state and district offices, and see how other charter schools are serving their students, what problems they have encountered, and how they are solving them.

Children may require special education services, occupational therapy, physical therapy, speech therapy, counseling, audiological services, medical services, adaptive equipment, and/or an in-class aide. Each of these children will have an IEP (individualized education program) specifying the services to be received, the providers of these services, their frequency, and the amount of time to be spent. Specific objectives will be set for each child. Intervention directed towards achievement of these objectives is to be both carried out and recorded. Likewise, progress is to be documented.

There are requirements as to how often the child's IEP objectives are to be reexamined and new ones set. There are also requirements as to the duration of the IEP and when new IEP's are to be developed. At this time the child must be reevaluated. This is to be done through a team process involving the child's teacher as well as all those involved in providing intervention. The parent is to be included in the IEP process. There are specific requirements as to parental rights and involvement, such as the number of days of advance notice of IEP meetings.

This is not to mention the complications of special education funding and the questions of liability that may arise if services are not provided in accord with the myriad of regulations.

You will need to decide whether you will have your district provide special education services or do just some of the services, such as conduct the IEP evaluations or meetings. Explore what additional staff you may want to hire or to contract for on a part-time basis. Determine whether your uncertified teachers or even certified teachers can perform services that under state regulation should be provided by teachers certified in special education (Schnaiberg, 1997, p. 25).

Other questions to be addressed include:

- Will the special education funding you receive cover the costs, and, if not, how can you secure full funding?
- Can you receive funding for children with special needs who come from outside your school district?
- Can the children with the most severe special needs be placed in district facilities other than your school?
- Can you cooperate with other charter schools in your area (McKinney, 1996, p. 25)?
- If you have individual learning plans for all your students, can parents waive their entitlement to conventional IEP's (Finn, Manno, and Bierlein, 1996, p. 55)?

Now is the time to research these issues and to be prepared for what may turn out to be an unexpectedly high population of children with IEP's.

Transportation

The first step in making your transportation decisions is to refer to your school's demographic profile:

- Will your students be coming from a relatively small, densely-populated urban area or will they be widely dispersed with long distances to travel?
- Will most of your parents have cars?
- Will parents be at work during the hours that the children must be transported?
- Will any of the transportation options preclude some parents from choosing your school?
- Will you be serving children with IEP's who will have special transportation needs?

You might be able to contract for bus service with your school district and spare yourself the worries of arranging for your own transportation. However, as pointed out above, this may impact your school's schedule, and it will not allow you to institute cost-saving measures. Further, if your students are coming from different school attendance areas, you will still have the hassle of making arrangements with the district bus service for pick-up points and times or perhaps for having a number of buses take the children to an existing alternative school and then transfer onto a bus which goes between that school and yours.

Is it feasible to use car pools? Your school can take on the responsibility of identifying for parents those other families in their area who will be attending as well as helping new parents contact existing car pools. The school should also determine the place outside the school where children will be dropped off and picked up, make sure that safety procedures are established and followed, and ensure that a child is not placed in a vehicle with a driver whom the child's parents have not approved. Parents who are unable to provide transportation may be able to provide other services, such as child care, to those car pool parents who transport their child.

Can your school take advantage of public transportation? Should you provide your own bus (or van) transportation? This has the advantage of allowing schools more freedom in scheduling the school day and also of having their own transportation for field trips. If you select this alternative, be prepared to provide insurance for your buses and drivers and make sure that your vehicle meets safety standards and is properly maintained. If staff members are to drive the vehicle, they will need to receive the training required to operate it.

Your school may choose a combination of these options, contract with a private carrier for transportation services, or just let parents handle their own transportation. Measure the pros and cons of your options, taking into consideration not only their relative costs, but also their implications for your educational program.

Food services

How will you provide for your students' school lunches? Check as to whether your state requires school provision of lunches. If not, sack lunches from home is one of your options. You may want to put restrictions on these lunches, e.g., no candy, no pop.

Your school might choose to use its district's lunch services with the food prepared in a neighboring school's kitchen. Your school would be responsible for maintaining a food count and collecting lunch money from its students. If it chooses to participate in the National School Lunch Program (NSLP), it will also be responsible for handling the forms from qualifying families.

Your school may choose to prepare and serve its own food. In this case it could also participate in the NSLP and follow all its procedures. In addition, it would be required to follow your area's public health and safety requirements. If your school chooses this option, it will need to have the equipment necessary for cooking, dish washing, etc. (Pioneer Institute for Public Policy Research, 1996, APP-I). It will also have to plan its menu, purchase food, and hire a cook.

This is one area where your school can be innovative. The Fenton Avenue Charter School in Lake View Terrace, California, one of the nation's largest, runs its own lunch program. As a result of using Marriott's catering service to evaluate its food service program, the school was able to save enough money to "purchase a new walk-in freezer and refrigerator, increase salaries of the food staff, add one full-time and one part-time staff person, and offer students more menu choices" (Finn, Manno, and Bierlein, 1996, p. 28). At the Minnesota New Country School a local restaurant has furnished hot lunches (Thomas, 1996, p. 22), and at the SciTech Academy in Littleton, Colorado different fast-food restaurants have brought in food, thanks to the efforts of a parent-student group (Abbott, 1994).

OTHER SCHOOL CONSTITUENCIES

Parents

Your organizational plan should include how you will both involve and enlist the participation of parents as well as foster parents, grandparents, and other family members. The section on parent ownership in Stepping Stone 7 describes ways in which parents can become involved through use of the school as a resource center and through a variety of volunteer opportunities. For your organizational plan you can pick and choose among these alternatives (or come up with your own) to arrive at those that will best serve your school's program and parent population. In addition, that section and Stepping Stone 6 describe how parent participation can be promoted through giving parents meaningful school ownership and creating a comfortable, supportive, challenging, rewarding, and enjoyable school atmosphere.

The question remains as to whether or not this participation should be required and, if so, how much and in which respects. You may want parents to commit themselves to making sure that their children attend school regularly, to attending parent meetings, to reading with their children, to helping them with their homework, to limiting their children's television watching, and/or to volunteering a specified number of hours or times (Amole, 1997; Becker, Nakagawa, and Corwin, 1995, p. 13).

Determine how parents will commit to participation:
- Will they verbally assent to participation?
- Will they commit themselves to involvement when they sign their children's application?

• Will they be required to sign a more structured parent contract (if contracts requiring parent participation in a public school are legal in your state)?

If you feel that parents will participate only if they sign a contract or like the concept of parents as contractual members of the school community, be aware that Becker, Nakagawa, and Corwin in their study of California charter school parent contracts concluded: "The overall tenor of the parent contracts used at most of the charter schools suggests that the contracts are viewed as a means of obtaining compliance rather than a positive vehicle for encouraging the growth of a more inclusive school community. These contracts, although probably intended to encourage more involvement, actually seem to permit schools more leverage over parents" (1995, p. vii). If you choose to use parent contracts, you may want to ensure that they involve obligations from both sides, that the school and the parent are, in fact, partners.

Staff

Former State Senator Gary Hart, the author of California's charter school legislation, stated in his closing address at the 1995 CANEC conference, "...one of the most fundamental aspects of charter schools that distinguishes a successful charter school, and one that is really having a significant impact, is that the charter school has to be able to control its own personnel decisions" (Hart, 1995).

This advice seems to have been heeded in Colorado where legislation does not allow an automatic waiver from public school laws and regulations, but establishes a procedure for seeking waivers from specific statutes. An evaluation of the state's first fourteen charter schools revealed that all of them had received a waiver from its Certified Performance Evaluation Act and thirteen had received a waiver from the Teacher Employment, Compensation and Dismissal Act. These waivers enabled the schools to achieve the autonomy to tailor their employment policies to their schools' educational approaches as well as, in the latter case, to have the opportunity to operate more economically (Clayton Foundation and Center for Human Investment Policy . . . , 1997, pp. 66-72).

Your educational program, including your decisions on the provision of special education and family services, will be a major determinant of your staffing needs. If you are a school established to serve children at-risk or with special education needs, you will have a greater need for support personnel. Financial considerations will be another important factor as you may choose to hire some staff members who are part-time, rely on extensive use of volunteers (if state law permits), and/or take advantage of "cross-utilized staffing arrangements" whereby staff perform more than one role (Mulholland and Bierlein, 1995, p. 33).

There are a number of other staff decisions which you must make. Will your staff be employees of your school, of your school district (considered as on leave of absence), or of another institution or company? In Colorado staff members of the Pueblo School for the Arts and Sciences are employees of the University of Southern Colorado, whereas the staff at the Community Prep School is employed by the City of Colorado Springs. Your state's legislation and your status as a separate legal entity, a conversion school, or an affiliate of another organization will determine or influence this decision.

If your school will be a conversion school, what rights

will your teachers retain? Will they be able to return to the district public schools? What about their benefits and the transfer of their years of service? You will need to work this out with your school district.

Other questions you will need to answer, always within the parameters of your state's regulations, include:
- Who will hire your staff?
- What job qualifications will you establish?
- Can you/will you hire uncertified teachers?
- Will you actively try to select an ethnically diverse staff?
- Who will process your payroll?
- Who will handle human resources responsibilities and be the contact person for your staff's employment questions?
- Will your staff have written contracts?
- Who will be involved in staff contract negotiations?
- What will be the length of staff contracts?
- Will your employees be at-will?
- What criteria will be established for contract renewal?
- What performance assessment will you use?
- Will you follow your district's pay schedule?
- What benefits will you offer (retirement, medical/dental insurance, life insurance, disability benefits, vacation leave, sick leave, funeral leave, maternity leave, family leave, personal days, employee assistance programs) and will they be comparable to those offered in your district?
- Will you, as in Michigan, be able to secure benefit packages through your state's charter school association (Michigan Association of Public School Academies)?
- What grievance procedure will you establish?
- Will your school be exempt from local labor-management agreements?

- Will your staff be able to choose to or continue to be members of a teachers' union? If so, how will this tie into your school policies, especially those on teacher certification, salaries, and benefits?

The employment policy which you adopt will undoubtedly affect union support of your school. The National Education Association's criteria for charter schools include the use of "licensed educators" and employment conditions "equal to those of educators and other employees in existing public schools" that "include tenure, due process, seniority, health insurance coverage, and, in accordance with existing state law, provision for coverage in the state teachers' retirement plan" (National Education Association, 1995, pp. 4–5).

Assess the attitudes of the unions in your area and, especially if a school district is to be your sponsoring agency, the strength of their relationship with the district (Premack, 1995, p. 4). When a group of teachers in Aurora, Colorado proposed a charter school, they encountered opposition from the union of which they were members on a number of issues, including the number of hours staff would work, not having a principal, and, especially, the proposed class sizes which would be smaller than those in the district's regular public schools. It took the school's organizers about two years to get approval from the union board (Interview with Robert Hamilton-Pennell, 1997). Be prepared for the union opposition which your employment policy may arouse.

Administrator

Referring to charter school administration, Finn, Manno, and Bierlein stated:

Successfully leading a charter school is arduous. It calls
for an uncommon blend of educational vision, administrative acumen, business savvy, political sophistication,
and public-relations adroitness (1996, p. 41).

Charter schools have used a number of unique leadership options. The Accelerated Charter School in Los Angeles
has codirectors (A Profile of California's Charter Schools,
1996, p. 60), and at the Hilltown Cooperative Charter School
in Haydenville, Massachusetts office duties are the province
of the administrator, while the teachers determine educational policy (Ponessa, 1996, p. 33).

If you follow the alternative of not hiring an administrator (and, thereby, saving money), who will assume the
responsibilities? You will have to come up with your own
unique arrangement. For instance, at the Constellation
Community Charter Middle School in Long Beach (enrollment of about 130), the staff consists of only five teachers
and two aides. The teachers estimate that they put in an extra
five to eight hours a week performing administrative duties.
One is responsible for purchasing and parent involvement,
one is in charge of community relations and maintenance,
while a third has assumed responsibility for the payroll, student activities, and governing board meetings, etc. Together
the teachers meet weekly to make decisions that range from
holiday parties to elective courses (Ponessa, 1996, pp.
28–30). You may wish to contact other charter schools which
have no administrator.*

Regardless of whether you decide to follow the more
prevalent charter school practice of hiring a director or adopt

*Throughout this book those who assume administrative responsibilities will,
when exercising those responsibilities, be referred to as the administrator.

a different approach, you will need to insure that the individual or the team as a whole possesses the combination of necessary administrative qualities. First, of course, you must assure that the administrator is in complete accord with your school's educational program (including its mission). The members of your organizing committee should fit this bill, and undoubtedly at least one of them is displaying leadership and visionary qualities in driving your charter school's application process. Does this make him/her qualified to be your school's administrator?

A charter school is not only an educational venture, but also a business. Further, it is a business that is constrained by a very tight budget; that is accountable to its "customers" (its parents), its "licensor" (its sponsoring agency), and its "payors" (the taxpayers); that is operating in largely uncharted territory; and that is subject to continuing public scrutiny. Do not assume that the individual who will deserve the lion's share of credit for making your charter school a reality can also make it a success.

Carefully establish the qualifications for your administrator position. If you are restricted by state regulations, see if you can follow the example of the eleven of Colorado's first fourteen charter schools who secured a waiver from the state's statute on the employment and authority of principals (Clayton Foundation and Center for Human Investment Policy . . . , 1997, p. 72). Decide how much and what kind of experience you would require. Do you want to hire someone from within your school district who is already familiar with the district board and central office personnel (and procedures), a quality which may be valuable as you establish relations with them during the preoperational and operational periods? Determine which functions your administrator will perform and write a job description for that person.

Once again, you will need to establish a recruitment/hiring process and decide upon your administrator's salary, benefits, assessment, etc.

Governing board

"Poorly-specified and executed governance designs are fast becoming a major internal (and later external) problem for charter schools"—so states CANEC's Characteristics of Strong Charter Petitions, which were approved by its board of directors in January 1997 ("CANEC's Characteristics . . . ", 1997, p. 5).

Governance problems can have widespread repercussions not only by impeding decision-making, but also by creating oppositional factions in the school community which, if unchecked, can adversely affect morale, school image, and your students.

In setting up your governing board, your first step should be checking on your state's charter school statute to see if there are any specific requirements. Those persons often serving on governing boards are teachers, administrators, parents, and community members. In addition, some governing boards include students and representatives from those organizations with which they are affiliated. At The EXCEL School in Durango, Colorado, the board does not include the administrator or any staff because it is designed to be a "policy board" that does not "micromanage" (Interview with Ballantine, 1996). Choose the composition that is best suited to your governance philosophy and that will facilitate decision making. For instance, a board composed of equal numbers of parents and staff with no outside member is ripe for deadlock (Wilson, 1997).

You will need to decide how board members are selected and the length of their terms. Boards whose membership terms are "for life" and those with only a small percent of elected members may not have the same incentive to be responsive to the school community. On the other hand, if all your board's members come up for election at the same time, there may be a tendency to overrespond to the situation of the moment and less continuity in governing policy. Determine the length of your terms and whether they will be staggered or rotating (so that if someone resigns before the end of a term, the new member can serve a full rather than the uncompleted term). Specify how your initial board will be chosen or provide the names of those already selected (Premack, 1997b, p. 21). Also, decide whether you wish to have a procedure for member recall.

It is crucial that you spell out the responsibilities of the governing board, in general terms now and through more detailed bylaws during the preoperational period. Will the board, the administrator, the teachers, or a combination thereof be responsible for your school's key decisions? Carefully delineate in writing the division of responsibilities and make sure that they are communicated to all the school's stakeholders. Do your utmost now to avoid later dissension both between and within your school's constituent groups.

SITE AND SITE SUPPORT

Site selection

If you are a conversion school, you are indeed fortunate in this regard. You already have your school site and except for perhaps renovations to adapt it to your new educational program, you are basically set. If you are instead to be a "from-scratch" school, begin immediately to find a school location. Even if your sponsoring agency does not require a site in-hand before charter approval, it will want to know what options you are considering and what progress you have made. Site selection is often a time-consuming, drawn-out process and has been the downfall of some charter applicants. Make it a high priority.

Your best site is probably a school building. These buildings are already designed for school operation and located where there will be no zoning problems. Check with your school district for possible sites. Does it have a vacant school building? Will the building have to be brought up to code or remodeled to meet Americans with Disabilities Act requirements? Does it meet your needs as to size, neighborhood, etc.? In Denver use of the Crofton Elementary School building was turned down by one charter school applicant because it was not located in the lower downtown area that was tied into its school mission ("P.S. 1 Rejects...", 1995), while another applicant was wary of the drug traffic and crime in its neighborhood and of the additional security costs which might be incurred (Stevens, 1995).

If the school district cannot provide you with an appropriate building, embark on an extensive search. Although you will probably have a site selection subcommittee, recruit all of your organizing committee members in this effort. Each member should be on the lookout for possibilities in his/her neighborhood and network with friends and acquaintances.

Your site selection subcommittee will want to work with a real estate agent. Also, do your own pavement pounding,

Table 7	Charter School Sites*
Apartment building	Office building
Business park	Parochial school
Church	Recreation center
City building	Restaurant
College or university campus	School within existing school
Convent	Social service agency
Department store	Strip mall
Elks lodge	Supermarket
Living room and garage	VFW building
Military building	YMCA
Mill	YWCA
Modular classrooms	

* In a number of cases these sites are listed by their earlier use.
Source: Abbott, 1994; Anderson, 1994; Commonwealth of Massachusetts, Department of Education, 1997b, pp. 18–36; Grantier, 1995; Lange et al., 1996, p. 9; Nathan, 1996, pp. 54, 163; Ponessa, 1996, p. 28; Wallis, 1994, p. 53; Weiss, 1997, pp. 25–27.

use the media to keep aware of legal motions and business closings, and continue to network (Pioneer Institute . . . , 1996, p. VI-2). Don't restrict yourself to the obvious. This is an opportunity to be creative. Table 7 lists some of the sites which charter schools have chosen.

To evaluate a site you must first know your estimated enrollment, the number of classrooms and offices you will need, and whether you are planning to have an on-site library, computer laboratory, lunchroom, parent lounge, gymnasium, playground, athletic fields, etc. How large a parking area will you need? Will you need space for warehousing?

Does a potential site meet these needs? If not, are there nearby facilities which you can use? For instance, according to the evaluation of Minnesota charter schools, "Many programs are taking advantage of community-based resources (the public library, recreational facilities, public playgrounds, neighboring school cafeterias, a YWCA) to overcome potential inadequacies" (Lange et al., 1996, p. iii).

Other questions you may need to consider include:

- How much traffic is in the area of a potential site?
- Is it close to your intended population?
- If you would be sharing your facility with another organization, will you be able to schedule joint usage so as not to disrupt your educational program?
- If you are displacing another facility user, such as a senior center, what opposition will you encounter?
- How receptive is the neighborhood to your school?
- If you plan to expand, will the facility be adequate or will you need once again to go through the site selection process?
- Do you want multiple campuses?

You will, of course, need to check zoning restrictions. Make sure there is no asbestos in the building, that it is safe structurally, and that it meets fire code regulations. The amount of needed renovation will be a crucial factor. Get input from your building inspector as to what will be required and come up with some figures. For instance, the Community Involved Charter School in Lakewood, Colorado, which is located in a church, discovered that, in addition to a $30,000 water and sewage tap fee, its expenses included:

Lower level fire and sprinkler system $26,255
Fire/smoke alarm system, all levels   25,885
Architectural code analysis   2,712
Environmental study   5,000
Security system   9,175
Colorado public safety inspection fee   400
Local government site plan/architect fee   200
Application fee   100
(Sweeney and Garcia, 1995, p. 2.)

How much can your expenses can be reduced through "sweat labor"? At the Sci-Tech Academy in Littleton, Colorado the work of teachers, parents, and students in remodeling a K-Mart store saved the school about $80,000 (Abbott, 1994). Can your renovations be handled by volunteers or will you need to contract for them? Be sure to check on local regulations and union rules.

Contact your state department of education as to whether any funds are available for meeting ADA requirements or for asbestos removal (Nathan, 1996, p. 162) and whether any federal grant or state funding is available for charter school capital costs. Some states are considering arrangements for assisting with charter school capital needs.

The bottom line, however, is that capital funds are generally not available from school districts; that, unlike your school district, you cannot issue bonds; and that you will probably find it difficult to secure a loan. Rexford Brown of Denver's P.S. 1 found his group's loan-seeking efforts caught in the trap of no charter, no loan—no loan, no charter. The school did, however, secure $90,000 in borrowed funds: $15,000 from the landlord to be paid back from the lease and a $75,000 six year loan from the Gates Foundation (Interview,

1997). If you are unable to secure such financing, you may well end up following the example of other charter schools which finance facilities with operating funds (Finn, Manno, and Bierlein, 1996, p. 34).

Your site expenses, even apart from renovation, will be a major factor in determining the financial viability of your school. These costs may be as high as 15 percent of your operating budget ("Colorado Charter School . . . ", 1996, p. 4). It will be difficult enough to operate your school on what is often less than the funding of a comparable public school without shouldering this continuing burden.

In securing a facility, you will have the choice of renting, leasing, or, if they are legal options in your state, buying or leasing with an option to buy. Whichever you choose, a major objective of your site subcommittee should be not spending more than you have available.

Stepping Stone 10 discusses the pursuit of new funding sources and arrangements. This is important not only during, but also before your school's operation and especially in financing a site. Work closely with your subcommittee(s) that deals with marketing and fund-raising. Find a fairy god-mother (or godfather), perhaps a college, university, city, or church, from whom you can lease a facility below market price, for a $1-a-year fee, free of charge, for only the utility payments, etc. If you need to, delay the submittal of your charter application until you have found a site which meets both your program and financial needs.

Site Equipment

The list of equipment you may need and/or want for your school includes furniture (for both classrooms and offices), office equipment, computers, audiovisual equipment, and musical instruments. Actively seek the donation of what you need and go to thrift stores, garage sales, and estate sales. You may be able to secure low cost furniture and office equipment from your state's surplus property agency ("Useful Tidbits", 1994, p. 3). Make sure that the equipment you receive is usable (for instance, that there is still software available for the computers).

Site support

Determine whether your groundskeeping, custodial, security, and maintenance services will be provided in-house or by the school district, outside contractors, or volunteers. This is one area in which you may be able to secure substantial savings.

ADMINISTRATION

Sections of your application dealing with the administrator and the governing board have been discussed above. There are other issues, however, which relate to your school's administration.

Financial operations

Who will be responsible for:
• making purchases;
• writing checks;
• keeping your books;
• getting out your payroll checks and handling other employee benefits;
• keeping track of your revenue and expenditures and, in so doing, monitoring your budget; and
• assuring internal controls?

You will need someone with know-how and experience to set up and/or assume these responsibilities.

Your staff may be employees of a college, university, city, foundation, or some other organization which will include your school in its financial systems. You may wish to contract with one of these organizations or an accountant to provide these services. Your school district will be knowledgeable in dealing with the complexities of public school finance. This is one area in which you might wish to use its services, but, here again, you will need to determine whether this is the most economical or wisest route. You may also choose to have an accountant or bookkeeper on staff.

Financial accountability

Your school needs to be accountable financially. Check on your state's audit requirements and, as recommended by Premack for those California charter schools not receiving school district financial services, "establish the audit standards, scope, and auditor selection process early in the development of the charter school and clearly specify the scope and timing of the annual audit in the charter document" (1997a, p. 49).

Performance accountability

Your school also needs to be accountable performance-wise. Methods of measuring student progress have been discussed in the student assessment section above. Determine what accountability reports are required by your sponsoring agency. Ways of demonstrating accountability include:
- attendance rate,
- dropout rate,
- suspension/expulsion rate,

- graduation rate,
- percentage of college-bound students,
- surveys of parent, staff, and student satisfaction, and
- accreditation.

Other areas

There are other administrative areas which should be covered in your organizational plan. In your plan specify the areas in which you will be addressing health and safety procedures, e.g., motor vehicles; emergencies such as fires, tornadoes, and earthquakes; immunizations; contagious diseases; dispensing medicines; handling body fluids and chemicals; and machine safety.

Stepping Stone 3 suggested ways of addressing political issues. Through the process of gaining allies for your school, you have been developing a public relations program, focusing on the need for your school, and securing community support and involvement, all areas which are important to your application. You may also be required to, or wish to, include a founding coalition profile (names of your organizing committee members, their backgrounds, partnership arrangements, etc.) in your application.

If you are required to, address relations with your school district, pointing out what contacts you have made and the communication procedures and operational arrangements you will be establishing.

From the time of your earliest meetings you have established record-keeping procedures. These written records will be invaluable not only to your school, but also in meeting your state's replicability requirement.

LEGAL ISSUES
••••••••••••••••••••••

Many of the decisions which you have been making have legal ramifications. In addition, you will need to make sure that your school complies with open meeting statutes, the Americans with Disabilities Act, federal civil rights laws, etc. Two legal issues which you will also need to address are legal status and liability/insurance.

Legal status

State laws vary widely as to the legal status of charter schools. Under a model charter school law, charter schools would be not only fiscally, but legally autonomous (Vergari and Mintrom, 1996, p. 5). You may live in a state where all charter schools are legally autonomous independent cooperative and/or nonprofit entities. In others, charter schools are part of a school district with varying degrees of independence as determined by their charters. In still others, the legal status of a charter school and the extent of its autonomy depends on the sponsoring agency selected. You will need to have legal advice in determining your state's requirements; in deciding, if there is a choice, which option is preferable for your school; and in negotiating the optimum degree of autonomy in your charter.

In any event, you will want to apply immediately for non-profit status so that, among other reasons, you may accept donations (Nathan, 1996, p. 125). You might also consider setting up a not-for-profit foundation (Commonwealth of Massachusetts, Executive Office of Education, 1996, p. 14). Here again take advantage of legal counsel.

Liability/insurance

Your potential liability will be affected by the state in which your charter school is located and your legal status. You will need to have liability insurance for your employees, your governing board, and possibly your classroom volunteers as well as insurance on your property (facility and vehicles) and worker's compensation.

You may be able to participate in your school district's insurance coverage or join with other charter schools to secure coverage (BW Associates, 1994b, p. 18). There may be the possibility of tying in to a state-operated or state school board association insurance program (Nathan, 1996, p. 162). The Michigan Association of Public School Academies offers its charter school members the opportunity to participate in a property, liability, and worker's compensation insurance program (Michigan Association of Public School Academies). Buying insurance in the open market is always an option. This is an area in which you will need to seek advice from your accountant and your attorney.

BUDGETS

Looking at the first year in which California charter schools were operating, Dianda and Corwin reported, "Forty-four percent of the schools, including most new starts, found that lack of funding was a major obstacle in creating a charter school" (1994, p. 58).

According to the schools surveyed in the National Study of Charter Schools, "lack of start-up funds" and "inadequate operating funds" were, respectively, the first and third greatest barriers they encountered (RPP International and University of Minnesota, 1997, p. 35).

A charter school cannot succeed unless it is economically viable. Regardless of the merits of your program, the satisfaction of your parents, and the fulfillment of all the goals in your mission statement, your efforts will come to naught if your school cannot succeed financially.

As you have been developing your application, you have been feeding your cost options/estimates (including the capital funding needed for your building renovation) into an emerging budget. Once the other portions of your organizational plan are almost completed, you will need to finalize your budget or, more appropriately, budgets, so that they may be included in your application submittal. In fact, however, your budgets will never be finalized. Throughout your preoperational and operational periods, you will constantly need to reexamine and revise your budgets to reflect changes in your actual and anticipated revenues and expenditures and to make sure they are in alignment.

Include the three budgets discussed below in your organizational plan. The budget documents should be prepared by your financial expert; each item should be carefully reviewed by each member of your organizing committee; and the budgets should be finalized only when your organizing committee has reached a consensus. Remember that your budget is the tangible expression of your school's mission. Conflicting opinions on both your mission statement and your budget should be resolved before your application is submitted.

Start-up budget

Your start-up budget will be the budget which covers the preoperational period of your school. Determine which of your estimated expenditures you will be incurring during this period. You may want to plan for enough funds for your staff to be on board early (Weiss, 1997, p. 14). You will be including such items as the costs of supplies and equipment, marketing, your telephone, and perhaps rent. The funding of building renovation, discussed in the section on site selection, will also be included in this budget.

Since your school is not yet operational, you will not be receiving any per pupil operational or categorical funds. You will probably have to scrape hard to cover your start-up costs, and your difficulties may well be compounded by cash flow problems. Anticipate these problems and take appropriate steps now.

See if your state offers any start-up funding. Buechler reported in his January 1996 study that only Arizona, Georgia, Massachusetts, and New Mexico offered these funds (pp. 9–10) and pointed out that "the amount they provide is small compared to the expense of getting a school up and running" (p. 30). Also, check with your state as to whether U.S. Department of Education Public Charter Schools grant money is available. In fiscal year 1996 Minnesota charter schools secured federal planning/start-up grants ranging from $9,000 to $50,000 (Lange et al., 1996, p. xiii). This is an area in which charter school proponents are advocating assistance, so keep abreast of the latest developments in your state.

Use fund-raising to secure start-up revenues, being sure to check on fund-raising restrictions in your state. Stepping Stone 10, which describes some of the assistance other schools have received, may offer some suggestions which will be applicable to your situation.

Be aware that in your preoperational and early operational periods you may encounter problems caused by delays in receiving your funding. According to Bierlein and Fulton, "For small, start-up charter schools, such cash flow issues are significant. For example, Michigan's fiscal year begins

October 1, although most schools begin in August. This means that schools in Michigan do not receive their first state-aid payment until mid-October. Most districts have funds remaining from the previous year, but new start-up charter schools do not" (1996, p. 26).

Conversion schools may also have cash flow problems if the funds they receive initially are based on their previous year's smaller enrollment (a problem which also may be faced later by expanding charter schools) (Little Hoover Commission, 1996, p. 92).

Try to secure a short-term loan from your sponsoring agency (p. 92); if possible, avoid having to mortgage your home as did a couple at Lansing, Michigan's Sankofa Shule charter school (Pearson, 1996); but by all means, make sure you can cover your expenses.

Operating budget

You will also need to come up with a budget for your school's first year of operation. Although for your school's purposes, you will have separate start-up and operating budgets, items in your start-up budget that were received or spent during the first fiscal year in which your school was operating must be included in that year's operating budget in your official reports (Pioneer Institute . . . , 1996, p. VII-5).

Long-range operating budget

During your first year you will be incurring many one-time expenses. It is necessary for you to determine whether your school will be doing better financially in later years and whether, with time, it will be economically viable. You will want to factor in the effects of expansion, your plans to move to a different facility, etc. Come up with a long-range operating budget that will cover at least the term of your charter.

Stepping Stone 5

....

If Your Application Is Rejected, Activate Plan B; If Approved, Negotiate a Charter Which Meets Your Priorities and Prepare for Start-up

The moment of truth. The moment you've been anticipating, yet dreading. Will your application be approved? If
not, what will you do? If it is, what will you do? This stepping stone discusses the in-between time, the time between
the framing of your charter application and the start-up of
your school.

CHARTER PRESENTATION
••

Your presentation date is imminent. You have prepared
(and agreed upon) the first draft of your organizational plan and
incorporated all or part of it into your application. You have
enlisted community support and gotten to know each member
of your sponsoring agency. What more should you do?

Circulate your application for review. Include representatives of all those segments of the community who support
your efforts and perhaps some of your opponents. Submit it
to the staff of your sponsoring agency and/or school board. If
your sponsoring agency has a committee which makes an initial review and recommendation to the agency board, submit
it to that committee. Carefully consider the feedback and, if
necessary, come up with a revised application.

Remember that if your sponsoring agency is your school board, it may be reluctant to acknowledge that it is not meeting the needs of all its students, may be worried about the financial viability of your school, may not want to give up its power, and may not be supportive of the charter school law. Be prepared, insofar as possible, to show that your school is "a win-win" for the district (Interview with Hamilton-Pennell, 1997), that it will fill a niche that is not being served, that the community wants it, that it will boost the district's image, and that it will not be a financial drain. Try to address the concerns of each board member.

Consider which persons will be your most effective presenters and will have the most clout. Choose a primary spokesperson. If an attorney has been a part of your organizing committee, include him or her in your presentation group.

Then practice your presentation. Get feedback on the organization of your presentation, its length, etc. Enlist several persons as devil's advocates and become comfortable and adept in countering their arguments (Nathan, 1996, p. 137).

Keep in touch with individual board members so that you get a feel as to their support. It is better for you to delay your presentation than to be turned down.

Bring letters of support with you to the presentation. Prepare a list with brief bios of your organizing committee members. Also, see if you can submit a summary of your proposal prior to the meeting (Premack, 1997b, p. 39).

Among the suggestions offered by Premack for the meeting itself was, "Allow the board members to let off steam as some board members feel a need to grandstand for their constituents or to appear extra vigilant in the review process." Answer every question and, above all, keep your cool (1997b, pp. 39–40). You will also want to have supporters present at the meeting.

PLAN B
••••••••••••

If despite your best efforts your proposal has been turned down or the odds are currently against you, what do you do next?

Before you presented your application, you looked at your options and pretty much decided what you would do in this eventuality. Now is the time to revisit your Plan B.

Begin by soul-searching, individually and as a committee. Perhaps the process has taken several years, you have been turned down more than once, there is only one chartering agency, and/or some of the children of your organizers have become too old to attend the school. Will enough key members remain on your organizing committee? Is the enthusiasm and drive still there? Have you received some encouragement that your application is potentially acceptable? Is it wise to continue? If the answer is yes, consider your options.

Appealing

If your state's legislation provides for appeals, investigate its appeals process:

- Could the appeal board require the sponsoring agency to reconsider its decision or would it have the authority to overturn it?
- What appeal procedure would you need to follow?
- How successful have appeals been in your state?
- How much time would there be between the appeal board's decision and your school's opening?

If you decide to appeal, carefully examine the reasons your application was turned down by your sponsoring agency. Were they political? Did they relate to your presentation and/or the application itself? Decide whether you can make a strong enough case to overturn the ruling. Enlist legal advice. Have some of those who were present critique your earlier presentation and benefit from their comments. Determine the best approach for addressing the appeal board. Once again, practice your presentation.

Delaying

Another option is to delay. This will give you time to strengthen your application, incorporate those suggestions from your sponsoring agency with which you feel comfortable, and gather more support, both in the community and among sponsoring board members. Can you extend the application deadline? If so, would there be enough time between approval and your start-up date? You might consider delaying for a longer period and resubmitting the application with appropriate changes the next year. Will the composition of your sponsoring agency change in the interim? How feasible is the option to delay?

Applying to a different sponsor

Does your state's charter statute authorize more than one sponsoring agency? For instance, in Arizona charter schools can be sponsored by a school district, the state board of education, or the State Board for Charter Schools. Look at the track record of the various sponsoring agencies in your state. Even if charter schools in your state are sponsored only by school districts, you might be able to apply to a different district.

NEGOTIATION

Your charter may have been approved with the proviso that you fulfill certain conditions. Further, even though your charter has been approved, you will need to sign a chartering contract with your sponsoring district. Before you begin negotiations, determine your priorities. Which items are absolutely essential to your school's mission and not negotiable? On which items are you willing to compromise or concede?

Make sure that you clearly understand the terms of the charter and that it will enable you to carry out your plans. For instance, will you be able to contract for services? If it is a negotiable item, seek a length of term that will give your school sufficient time to achieve its goals.

PREOPERATIONAL PERIOD

Now is the time to get ready for the first day of school. Look back at the Stepping Stone 3 and 4 chapters. Continue to follow the Four E's. Flesh out your organizational plan, thereby converting it into a management plan, a working plan for your school's operation. Determine what you will need to accomplish before school starts—and then do it.

Expertise

Now that you have gone into business, you will really need expertise. Be willing to pay for it. Hire a topnotch administrator. Be very discriminating in choosing your teaching staff. Select mostly teachers who have experience (Nathan, 1996, p. 144), but be aware that novice teachers paired with master teachers may add a special dimension to your educational program. Above all, hire only those teachers who support your charter's mission.

A capable secretary/receptionist will do much to grease the wheels of your school's daily operation. If you have not already done so, select, contract with, or establish relations with a special education teacher, a bookkeeper, an auditor, a bank, etc., making sure that each is highly competent and has relevant experience. Capitalize upon the various talents of your parents. Make sure that your governing board has expertise in all relevant areas (Premack, 1997b, p. 47).

Efficiency

The report on the Seattle charter school workshop points out that "with the hiring of paid staff, governance of the charter school shifts from a more or less consensual arrangement between members of the core team and other volunteers to a series of hierarchical and contractual relationships..." (Millot and Lake, 1996, p. 30). This is the time when the shift occurs. During this period the core team will be gradually relinquishing its decision-making and implementation responsibilities to those hired to assume them.

Your management plan will be the written instrument through which you establish these hierarchical and contractual relationships. It will divide responsibilities among your school's constituent groups and establish chains of accountability.

Begin to implement your management plan by hiring someone with management capabilities, either from your organizing committee or elsewhere, to be a stand-in administrator until your permanent administrator is on board. Also hire a secretary, who will work closely with the interim administrator, establish office systems, and become intimately familiar with the school's set up. Then make selection of an administrator your highest priority.

Until you have hired the personnel to assume specific responsibilities, continue to utilize the subcommittees you have set up and establish any new ones you may need.

Finally, continue to keep your calendar, your timeline, your record keeping, and your budget up to date.

Effectiveness

Establishing an efficient system for transforming your "paper" school into reality should do much to assure the effectiveness of your efforts.

Enterprise

It is the spirit of enterprise which has gotten you where you are. Continue to cultivate it and look for it when you choose those who will become part of your school.

Educational program

- Mission statement: You no longer need to develop your mission statement. However, you face the equally important task of making sure that everyone involved with the school is both familiar with it and committed to the vision and goals it embodies.

- Outcomes, curriculum, student assessment: You will need to break down the goals for each grade level and domain into specific objectives; secure, revise, and/or write the curriculum which you want to implement; and determine your assessment tools. It is crucial that the work in this area be largely completed before school starts. Teachers will have enough to do in teaching their students and possibly assuming various administrative responsibilities without having to develop their curriculum and assessments at the same time. As teachers come on board, include them in the deliberations of the subcommittee(s) which has been working in this area, thereby familiarizing them with your mission and giving them a voice in developing the materials they will use. As in other areas, once the staff is hired, the subcommittee should bow out.

Students and student services

- Recruitment: Refine and implement your recruitment plan, targeting it to the students you have been established to serve. Develop an application form and a school brochure. Designate someone to meet with prospective students and their parents. Establish a student record-keeping system.

- Orientation: Plan for and implement your orientation program for new students and their families, e.g., home visits, an open house.

- Behavior code: Continue development of a behavior code that both conforms to your school's mission and assures a secure environment for everyone in your school. Make sure that it clearly specifies behavioral expectations and consequences. Spend time sharing it with prospective students and parents.

- Special education: Keep track of your latest student enrollment so that information on those children who are at-risk or have IEP'S can be used to determine your staff requirements. Establish contacts with those persons in your school district who are responsible for special education. Further familiarize yourself with special education financing, requirements, and procedures.

- Transportation: Prepare and keep handy a list of student addresses. Implement your transportation system: determining bus pick-up points, setting up car pools, etc.

- Food services: Make arrangements for your food services. Decide whether you will be serving snacks and, if so, how they will be provided.

Other school constituencies

In a study of five Massachusetts charter schools, Weiss concluded, "The most significant barrier within governance concerns role definitions and decision-making. Many school leaders and teachers are unsure of their job descriptions...and the parameters of their jobs. Which responsibilities are theirs, and which belong to the board? Who should be setting policies? What policies are to be classroom policies, and which are to be school-wide? How can collaborative decision-making be implemented efficiently" (1997, p. 11)?

In defining roles, you will first need to spell out the responsibilities of your governing board. Determine the policy areas in which your governing board should have authority and then assign other responsibilities, remembering that within a charter school they are often shared among different school constituencies. For instance, a Goldwater Institute survey of charter school teachers in Arizona revealed that 31% of the discipline policies were established by the director/superintendent, 10% by the teachers, 4% by an assistant director, and 53% by varying combinations of the director, assistant director, teachers, parents, and/or students (Gifford and Keller, 1996, p. 30). Attendance, text selection, grading, and teacher contract negotiation policies are examples of the many areas in which decision-making responsibilities must be determined (pp. 31–34).

In addition to the delineation of responsibilities, there are other tasks involving school constituencies which should be addressed during the preoperational period.

• Parents: Prepare a parent or parent-student handbook. If your school plans to use one, write a parent contract. In your meetings with prospective parents, listen carefully to their expectations from the school, secure information on the individual needs of each of their children, and make sure that they are fully informed as to the school's program and their roles in it. Involve parents in volunteer work projects, such as getting the building and grounds ready for start-up. Include parents in your orientation program. Schedule parent meetings. Prepare and distribute to parents a school calendar and the forms necessary for their children's enrollments (emergency cards, school lunch program forms, etc.).

- Staff: Determine your staff requirements and write job descriptions, keeping in mind the qualities you are seeking, e.g., experienced, innovative, enthusiastic, openminded, a team player, knowledgeable, committed, reliable, flexible. Advertise for staff members and decide whether you will wait for your administrator to be on board before making final staff decisions. Set the date on which staff should report, making it, within budget constraints, early enough for staff orientation, staff input into the educational program, and staff participation in student/family orientation activities. Prepare an employee handbook. Plan and conduct preoperational period staff development sessions and schedule staff development and planning times for the school year. Formulate your staff assessment procedures and determine how frequently reviews will occur.

- Administrator: Balance the advantages of hiring an administrator as soon as possible with the necessity to hire the right person. Carefully prepare a job description for your administrator position, detailing specific responsibilities and qualifications. (See Stepping Stone 4 for a discussion of the qualifications.) Conduct a job search.

When your administrator is on board, be supportive, but, from the beginning, let your administrator be in charge of his/her responsibilities.

- Governing board: Set up your initial governing board. You may want to have a "balance" of "a motivating force, the person(s) with the idea for the school; legitimized opposition; and a mediator" (Millot and Lake, (1996, p. 33) and/or a combination of "visionaries and pragmatists" (Interview with Mani, 1996). Study the workings of private school boards and the boards of nonprofit organizations and make arrangements for board member training. Adopt bylaws, establish working committees, and make sure that your meetings conform with legal requirements.

Site and site support

- Site: If you have not already done so, select your site. Do necessary renovations so that the site is ready for school occupancy. Acquire the equipment you need and set up your classrooms and offices.
- Site support: Make arrangements for groundskeeping, custodial, security, maintenance, and garbage pickup services.

Administration

- Within your school: Set up your bank accounts, your purchasing and payroll systems, and your human resources, internal control, and audit procedures. Develop a risk management policy, obtain insurance, set up your emergency procedures (including a handbook for the staff), buy first aid supplies, and get training for your vehicle drivers. Buy office and classroom supplies. Decide which staff committees you will need and set up a rotation schedule for such tasks as putting out playground equipment and cleanup of the staff lounge.

- School relationships: Make arrangements for interscholastic student activities, such as sports teams. Establish needed contacts between staff members and their counterparts in your school district. Maintain continuing contact between your administrator and the board of your sponsoring agency. Pursue your public relations program, both to aid in your recruitment of students and staff and to strengthen community support.

Legal issues

Secure incorporation and/or non-profit status. Carefully monitor your procurement policies, your meetings (to make sure that they conform to open meeting requirements), and your hiring of or contracts with members of your organizing committee (to avoid conflicts of interest) (Millot and Lake, 1996, pp. 7–8). Make sure that your student recruitment is nondiscriminatory, especially with respect to students with IEP's. Keep the school informed as to legal requirements and secure legal assistance as needed.

Budgets

Cash flow, capital funding, and your start-up budget will be of special concern during this period. Keep on top of what is happening, pursue cost-saving financial arrangements, and intensify your fund-raising efforts.

Stepping Stone 6

....

Create a Learning/Working Environment Which Is Comfortable, Supportive, Challenging, Rewarding, and Enjoyable

You have spent months working on the nuts and bolts of your charter application and your management plan. You have been busy gathering support for your school, securing expert advice, and finding a site. You are engaged in a host of start-up tasks, including staff recruitment, student enrollment, and securing the necessary tables, computers, and office supplies. During this whole process you have felt the time pressure of deadlines: the charter application due date, perhaps the appeal date, and now the start-of-school date. And, throughout, you have been trying to be efficient and effective. In accomplishing all this, have you overlooked the learning/working environment of your school?

Every school has an atmosphere. The staff knows what it is, the students know, the parents know, and perhaps the community senses it. What kind of learning/working environment do you want for your school? Will you just trust that it will be a good one or will you take positive measures to create and maintain your school's atmosphere?

Each charter school's environment should be tied into its mission, the climate which it seeks to foster in carrying out its vision. You will want to decide what kind of environment is best for your school. A sense of school ownership, the topic of the next stepping stone, will be an important element in your school environment. The five qualities suggested here—comfortable, supportive, challenging, rewarding, enjoyable— would probably be regarded as desirable characteristics in any charter school, regardless of its mission.

Comfortable

Stress is inherent in working with children. Being a teacher to a group of children, some of whom present major learning and/or behavioral challenges and each of whom is unique in his/her personality, learning style, and background, makes teaching a stressful occupation. This stress is compounded in a charter school where staff members assume new, perhaps less clearly-defined roles and often are not acquainted with each other or with the school. Thus, it is all the more important that staff members feel comfortable in their working environment.

Stress can never be eliminated, but it can be reduced. Giving the administrator and the staff school ownership, implementing effective communication procedures, and reducing unrealistic time demands are ways of decreasing stress which are discussed in the next three stepping stones. There will always be crises, large and small, but anticipating problems and planning ahead so they do not arise or will be dealt with through an established procedure can do much to eliminate a "crisis atmosphere" in your school.

Staff members also feel more comfortable when they are given respect: when each person's job is regarded as important, when the time stresses and challenges of their work are recognized, when their ideas and opinions are taken seriously and considered, when their accomplishments are acknowledged, and when they are trusted. When staff members feel secure and comfortable in their work environment, their assurance will be transmitted to their students.

Students and parents will likewise feel comfortable in your school when they know that they are important members of the school community, when their needs are recognized, and when they are accorded respect. Your administrator and staff should be aware that a special effort may be required to make your parents feel comfortable. According to the Minnesota Charter Schools Evaluation, "...since parents have no previous experience with the school, nor anyplace to turn to establish a sense of expectations about how it will work, there is often anxiety and concern..." (Lange et al., 1996, p. 61).

In addition, some parents had negative experiences when they went to school. They may have been from a minority group or from a family less well off than those of their peers, had learning difficulties, or been unhappy in an authoritarian classroom environment. Other parents whose children have had negative school experiences may have become quietly disgruntled with the school system or, as advocates for their children, encountered hostile reactions from school staff. Some parents whose children have experienced classroom success may have become dissatisfied with school policy and their inability to make changes. Still other parents may feel ill at ease when in the presence of professional teachers and administrators. You need to make these parents feel at home in your school.

Parent participation can best flourish in a school which welcomes them and values their input. Perhaps the most important factor in achieving such an environment is respect, shown to all parents. Really listening to parents' suggestions and criticism can in many cases help you better deal with their children.

In some schools staff members and administrators are called by their first names. You may feel that it is not respectful or conducive to discipline for children to address adults so informally. However, parents may feel more comfortable and as equal partners if they and the staff are on a first name basis.

Supportive

In organizing your charter school you needed to have the strong convictions and drive necessary to make your school a reality. In selecting staff and new governing board members, you have probably chosen a number of strong-minded leaders. Now that your school is operational and the inevitable controversial issues arrive, it may be especially difficult for your leaders to reach consensus or to be accepting of an administrator or staff member who does things somewhat differently than they would have done.

If your school is to function as a cohesive unit, there must be a spirit of tolerance and support, a respect for others' views and modi operandi. Staff development sessions and training workshops for your governing board should focus on conflict-resolution and team-building. Your governing board should resolve to be supportive of your administrator and likewise your administrator should make it a priority to be supportive of staff members, thereby setting the tone of the school.

Support should be available for all staff members. A procedure for handling classroom crises can be developed, more experienced teachers can serve as mentors, staff development meetings can focus on those areas in which staff members want help, and there should be opportunities for the staff to share information.

Likewise, the school needs to be supportive of parents,

readily answering questions and being parent-friendly, especially during conferences on student behavior and IEP staffings. Parents should be provided with helpful materials and referred to organizations which can assist them with specific problems.

Students can be supported by staff members who are open to their questions and concerns and who give them the extra time and assistance which they may need. Students can learn to be supportive of each other through such means as pairing older and younger students, group projects, reading buddies, partnering with those who have special needs, and fostering an environment where value is placed on helping others and recognizing their accomplishments.

Challenging

It is unlikely that you will have to come up with ways to challenge your governing board, your administrator, or your staff. They will face more challenges than they could ever bargain for.

Within the charter school there should also be challenging opportunities for parents. Table 8 on page 133 lists some parent volunteer options. Many of these options present opportunities for parents to exercise initiative.

Challenge is especially crucial for your students. According to the widely accepted theory of Jean Piaget, children's intelligence develops as it adapts to new information and perceptions. In order to learn, the information must be new, but not so advanced that the child cannot relate it to what he/she knows. In other words, children are not learning when they are bored by the repetition of what they already know; they learn when they must stretch to assimilate attainable knowledge. Staff members need to be aware of where each child is so that what is presented is challenging.

Rewarding

Being part of a charter school should be a rewarding experience. If the administrator, staff, parents, and students are given challenging tasks in a supportive environment, the accomplishment of these tasks should be personally satisfying.

In addition to intrinsic rewards, you should determine your school's policy on extrinsic rewards, a policy which will reflect your school's educational philosophy and preferences. Staff members will, of course, receive monetary compensation. What yearly pay increases and/or bonuses will be given? Will these take into account additional responsibilities and outstanding performance? Will students receive grades or smiley faces? What praise will be given? Do you want to write thank-you notes to parents, staff members, and students who have done something special? Will you have graduation ceremonies?

Finally, it is to be hoped that the successes of your school will bring the knowledge of "a job well done" to all those who are part of your school community.

Enjoyable

Is your school a happy school? Do your students and staff members like to come each day? Are they greeted warmly when they arrive?

Take time amidst all the daily demands to maintain a sense of lightness and humor and to plan some celebrations. These could be birthday parties, staff get-togethers, school-family picnics and outings to the roller skating rink, classroom celebrations of the first 100 days of school, bringing cookies for other staff members for no particular reason, and/or relaxing in the staff lounge.

You want your students to discover that learning is fun. Go out of your way to make the school experience enjoyable for everyone.

Stepping Stone 7

....

Foster a Sense of School Ownership in Your Students, Your Parents, Your Staff, Your Administrator, and Your Governing Board

What really matters for most of us are those things for which we have both responsibilities and input. Our families, our house or apartment, our car, our job, our church, our social relationships, our hobbies—in all these areas of our lives we feel a sense of ownership.

By their very nature charter schools lend themselves to this ownership. They are initiated and molded by individuals who go outside the established system to actualize their own educational mission. They not only encourage, but demand the time and efforts of a great number of participants. Each of you involved in the charter school application process rightfully experiences tremendous pride in the creation of "your" school.

Now that your school is operational, it is essential that this sense of ownership not only be maintained for you, its creators, but also, from the beginning, be extended to everyone involved in the school. It may be difficult to share the ownership, but as recommended in the Seattle charter school workshop: "The final phase is one of letting go. The applicant's leader and core team can't do it all" (Millot and Lake, 1996, p. 35).

The students, the parents, the staff, the administrator, the governing board—if each of these groups can come to feel it is their school, they will be more committed to its success. A source of friction, which has permeated some charter schools, will be alleviated, and you will discover that this commitment for yourself and from others will make a crucial difference in how you perceive and perform your job.

RESPONSIBILITY/EMPOWERMENT

When you developed your management plan, you divided responsibilities among the school's constituent groups. Now is the time to assign specific responsibilities. In assigning these responsibilities, consider who is qualified to perform the task, who is most concerned with the outcome, and how it will affect that person's overall workload. Likewise, the chain of accountability must be established.

From the beginning it is essential that both responsibilities and accountability for them should be clearly delineated and communicated. By so doing, conflicts among individuals as well as gaps in responsibility can be minimized.

In order to foster school ownership, each individual must be granted responsibilities which are meaningful. The person entrusted with a particular job (responsibility) should also be entrusted with the means to perform the job (empowerment). For example, if your teachers are responsible for the materials used in their classes within the limits of a set monthly expenditure, then they should be empowered to use the funds as they deem appropriate, e.g., making purchases, creating materials, using supplies from the school supply room, ordering through the school's catalogues, asking parents to donate shoe boxes, etc. If a teacher runs out of funds, underestimates the effort needed to create supplies, or fails to leave enough time to make adequate preparations, the teacher will have the incentive to adjust priorities and will experience personal satisfaction when the classroom's needs are met more efficiently.

This principle of ownership (responsibility plus empowerment) applies to all segments of the school community.

STUDENT OWNERSHIP

One can often sense the tenor of a school or a class in just a brief visit. When students truly "own" a school, the atmosphere will be a happier one, one with a sense of mutual respect and caring between teachers and students and among the students.

A number of charter schools have gone far towards establishing this ownership. According to Finn, Manno, and Bierlein, "The charter school was often described by students as a second family; indeed for some it was clearly the closest they had ever come to any sort of nurturing, caring family" (1996, p. 23). How can this ownership be achieved?

Prior to enrollment

Much can be done to encourage student ownership before the students' first day of school and even before their enrollment. When parents set up appointments to find out about the school, it can be helpful for their children to accompany them. From the beginning you will be stoking their interest in the school.

If your school is currently in operation, students will benefit from classroom visits. In some classroom situations the teachers may even allow visiting children to join in the activities. Familiarity with their teachers and the site will make it easier to make the school transition. They can visualize where they will be and have a feeling of anticipation that they will soon be part of the class. Even before they attend, your school has become their school.

In the interview with your school's representative, prospective students should be given an opportunity to peruse your school's brochure (even the nonreaders will enjoy the pictures) and to ask questions about the school's program. This is especially important if there is no opportunity for a site visit.

One charter school administrator has pointed out that some parents of older children are so eager to find an alternative to the school where their child is having problems that they don't really hear the descriptions of the school's program, discipline policy, etc. As a result, the parents may discover too late that they do not really subscribe to the school's philosophy and that their child doesn't fit into the program (Interview with Levine, 1996).

Children who are older may be more likely to observe the classroom with a critical eye, to hear what is being said, and to ask pertinent questions. They want to know about the programs in which they have special interests and about the amount of homework. These students may or may not have much impact on their families' school selection decision, but at least you have included them in the process.

Before school starts

Perhaps your school will have an end-of-the-year family party or picnic in which you can include students who are enrolled for the fall. Parents of the prospective students' classmates might call to invite a family and then serve as that family's host. Your staff and parents can welcome the family as members of the school community, and the students will have the opportunity to meet their classmates in an informal, fun-oriented activity. When school starts, they will see at least some familiar faces.

One way you might promote school ownership close to the start of the school year is a home visit for both new and returning students. Most students are excited when their teacher is coming to their home. This is true both for children who want to meet their new teacher and for children who will again see a teacher with whom they are acquainted.

Before you go on home visits, decide what you want to accomplish and what information you wish to convey. Be aware that you will be a guest in someone's home and that both a knowledge and appreciation of the family's culture will do much towards developing your relationship with the student and the family.

During home visits children may introduce their pets, demonstrate how they have learned to ride a two-wheeler, show off their toys or new school clothes, or serve cookies to the visitor. The teacher might encourage the children to talk about what they have done during the summer and what they would like to learn during the year. This is an opportunity for students to ask questions about your school or, if they are returning, about which of their friends will be in their room.

Expect that some children may be too shy or in awe to participate in the conversation. In some cases, the teacher may observe coordination problems, articulation difficulties, a high activity level, and/or hostility towards going to school. In each instance, the teacher has made a start towards understanding the child and towards making the classroom more attuned to individual needs. In addition, by visiting, the teacher is affirming the child, the child's family, and his/her everyday life as well as forging an important link between school and home.

The Clayton Charter School in Denver further fostered school ownership on the home visit by taking a photograph of each child and, in some cases, having the child draw a picture. When the children entered the room on their first day, they discovered that their photographs and/or pictures were displayed on the walls. The classroom was already their room.

In lieu of or in addition to the home visit, your school should hold an open house for parents and students. Children can see their classrooms, meet their teacher(s), and become acquainted with a few of their classmates (and parents can meet teachers and other parents, ask questions, and fill out any needed forms). Again, this is an opportunity for students to become familiar with their school before the often-scary first day.

When school starts

Teachers have always used a variety of methods to ease the transition to a new school or classroom. Name tags, individual cubbies or lockers, get-acquainted activities, school tours, and explanations of classroom rules, procedures, and expectations are just a few of the ways. A school-wide friendly atmosphere in which even the administrator and secretary give high priority to learning student names can also make students more quickly feel that it is their school.

During the school year

Now that you have done as much as you can to make the transition process an easy one, the hard work begins. The challenge of achieving a positive learning atmosphere lies in the day-to-day classroom experience.

Fostering student ownership should be a priority. Give your children assignments and projects (responsibilities) and ensure that they have the tools, such as materials, knowledge base, relevant experience, and teacher facilitation, (empowerment) to achieve success. This success can be acknowledged externally (good grades, teacher praise, peer regard) and/or internally (the satisfaction of knowing they have accomplished something worthwhile).

Students can be granted responsibilities which not only promote classroom achievement, but also contribute to the school. At The Connect School in Pueblo, Colorado, a middle school, students man the front desk and the telephone and, as there is only a part-time janitor, together with their teachers clean the school (Interview with Mikulas, 1996).

The students in the Constellation Community Charter Middle School in Long Beach review their school's budget. They are well aware of the relationship between their custodial duties and their school's new computers. They also realize that in California each day of a student's attendance adds about $20 to their school's funds, and they have attained a high attendance rate (Ponessa, 1996, p. 30).

The whole appearance of a school building, not to mention the pride of its students, is enhanced when student art work and stories are displayed on the walls. Dramatic presentations for parents and/or other classes, athletic teams, school choirs and bands, yearbooks, community service projects, letters to the media, and presentation of research recommendations to governing bodies can enable students to know that they are important members of their school community.

Culture building

Student ownership of your school can be attained only when it is "owned" by all your students including those students who are not "in the mainstream".

Rexford Brown has pointed to the need for "culture building" (Interview, 1997). If you can help your students buy into your school's culture, to subscribe to the school's mission, classroom stress will be reduced and learning enhanced.

To do so, you must first determine your school's culture. What are your major objectives? Are you striving towards high academic achievement, character development, cooperative learning, intrinsic motivation, emphasis on product or process, etc.? Students can subscribe to a school culture only if they know what it is.

During the application period framing and redefining your mission statement was a continuing priority. Since then new staff members have joined your team. Although they should already be committed to your school's overall philosophy, they are probably not familiar with specific objectives and the rationale behind them. Further, your goals must now be applied and adapted to the school's actual operations, to the new questions and challenges which are constantly arising. Take time to brainstorm the school's culture, to achieve staff consensus on basic objectives and procedures to apply in your classrooms.

How do you get students to share ownership of this culture? A number of students will, from the beginning, work towards what is expected of them. With the teacher as a mentor and a model they will strive to adapt to the classroom and achieve classroom goals. Given responsibilities and the tools to effect them, they will readily subscribe to the school's culture.

For others, the process may be more difficult, both for the student and the teacher. Data on student bodies from the sample schools in the Hudson Institute's charter school study revealed:

- More than half the students are eligible for free or reduced-price lunches.
- Almost one in five has limited English proficiency.
- Almost two-thirds are members of minority groups.
- Almost one in five has a disability or learning problem.
- Four percent had previously dropped out of school (and two percent were being educated at home) (Finn, Manno, and Bierlein, 1996, p. 30).

New charter schools may discover, as did one Colorado charter school, that whereas the parents of elementary-age children chose their school because of its educational program, the older students attending the school had been unhappy in their earlier school settings (Scanlon, 1996b). For a number of charter schools which were not established to handle at-risk students, the large number of these youngsters has posed major unexpected difficulties (Finn, Manno, and Bierlein, 1996, p. 31).

These students fall into several overlapping categories. Some students may have come from schools with completely different learning environments and find it difficult to adapt to your school. They may miss the friends and security of their old schools. These students will need support in adapting to their new environment.

Some of these students will evidence learning delays. Their old schools may not have covered academic areas which you take for granted or not have met your grade level standards. For these children, it is important to distinguish whether their difficulties are caused by inadequate preparation or by learning disabilities. If you have questions, it may be wise to have a classroom or special education teacher do an observation and, if the situation warrants, initiate the special education evaluation process.

For students to achieve school ownership, they must be given responsibilities and the means to achieve them. Students who cannot perform the classroom's work with their current capabilities will need support to maintain their self-esteem and to be given responsibilities which are within their reach. Likewise, they will need extra academic assistance.

At Colorado Springs' Community Prep School, which is designed to serve as a high-risk dropout retrieval program, some of the entering students are not prepared for the demanding curriculum. These students initially progress through competency-based computer-assisted programming to build their academic foundations (Interview with Rodriguez, 1997). Other schools offer tutoring and after-school programs to help students.

You have already determined whether special education services will be provided through the school or the district. Now you must look at your specific population of students with IEP's to define their needs. Do you need to increase your speech therapist's hours? Does the school need to hire its own special education teacher to supplement the district's intervention services? Do you need staff development sessions on detecting special needs?

The question of how these students' needs are to be met is also an important one. Should the special education teacher's role be one of consultation with the classroom teacher, provision of services within the classroom, or classroom pull-out intervention? Which alternative is most effective for each child and each classroom? With which alternative is the student most comfortable?

In those charter schools in which every student has an individual learning plan, is it necessary to single out these children? How can you keep these children from feeling different? What effort is the teaching team making to maximize the student's participation in classroom work and activities and to ensure that the classroom climate is one of acceptance and support?

There will also be students who bring to your school the negative experiences and feelings of their prior schools. Because as a charter school you have the flexibility and the dedication to the education of each student, you have a unique opportunity not just to cope with, but also to meet the needs of these troubled youngsters.

The paths you choose will depend on your individual situation. Perhaps you will arrange for extra security. Perhaps you will require school uniforms to prevent the display of gang colors (and increase school pride). Perhaps you will hire a counselor to work with individual students and classrooms. Perhaps you will provide family support services at the school. Perhaps you will modify or add to your curriculum. Perhaps you will negotiate individual behavior contracts between the student, the parent, and the teacher. Perhaps you will revise your suspension and expulsion policies. Perhaps you will institute conflict resolution training for both students and staff. Certainly you will discover each student's mode of learning and specific interests and tailor your teaching accordingly. And certainly, you and every one involved will spend hours brainstorming strategies.

Whatever options you choose, the best way to further student ownership is to give the students a stake in the process. Each student should be aware of the consequences of his/her actions and, if possible, help shape them. Even the youngest students should be present in at least part of parent-teacher progress or behavior conferences and have input in their behavior contracts. Conflict resolution procedures can include time for the protagonists to tell their side and reach a consensus on how to prevent a future occurrence. With training, second grade children can serve as conflict mediators.

Another group of students, those with limited English proficiency (LEP), will also need extra assistance. In developing your charter school proposal, you looked at the area's demographics. Plans should be in place to meet the needs of Spanish-speaking children or children from other non-English-speaking cultures. If not, this should be one of your highest priorities. At the Discovery Charter School, a K-6 school in Chula Vista, California, English-speaking children learn Spanish, while their Spanish-speaking classmates learn English ("A Profile...", 1996, p. 74). This is just one of many ways of making children with LEP feel a part of your school.

Regardless of whether your minority students speak English, teachers and other staff need to be attuned to their cultures. Minority staff members, staff development sessions, continuing affirmation of these children's families and heritages, and inclusion of a multicultural curriculum are among the means of fulfilling this objective.

Staff concern, respect, and acceptance; establishment of clearly defined expectations and consequences; avoidance of labels; and acknowledging accomplishments are crucial factors in dealing with all students. However, it is through granting students meaningful and attainable responsibilities that they can become full-fledged members of the school community.

PARENT OWNERSHIP

Charter schools are generally acclaimed for their parent involvement. Among the factors that may account for this participation are parent input in establishing the school, parent contracts that require parent participation, the opportunity for parents to participate in formulating school policy through governing boards, and parent belief in the school's mission and curriculum. Further, parents who are willing and able to participate may be the ones who more often select a charter school (Becker, Nakagawa, and Corwin, 1995, p. vii). Despite this parent involvement, the overall level of actual parent participation is low (p. 7). Moreover, Becker, Nakagawa, and Corwin suggest that "the message of many of these [parent] contracts seems to be that the parent is a consumer rather than a partner" (p. 21).

To succeed, charter schools need the support and commitment of their parents. This does not mean that parents should be micromanagers of your school. Management responsibilities have been established under your school's charter and by-laws and through administrative decisions. It is within this framework that parents need to become school stakeholders and partners.

A fit

As was the case for their children, there needs to be a fit between the parent and the school. Charter schools may in many cases be achieving this fit. The Goldwater Institute survey of Arizona charter school parents showed that 92% of them expressed satisfaction with their child's charter school and 94% were likely or very likely to reenroll their child (Gifford, 1996, pp. 16–17).

Nevertheless, schools need to be concerned with the minority of parents who are dissatisfied. Apart from the fact that these parents feel the school is not serving them and/or their children, a few unhappy and vocal parents can be draining to staff morale and create more widespread dissension. Some of this dissatisfaction should be welcomed as it raises legitimate issues which the school should address. Dissatisfaction stemming from parents' initial misconceptions about the school can be largely prevented at the outset. There are particular groups of parents who may need your special attention.

The Goldwater survey revealed that whereas only 1.6% of parents whose children had previously attended private schools were dissatisfied or very dissatisfied with the previous learning environment, 53.8% of parents leaving regular public schools for charter schools expressed dissatisfaction with their child's school experience (Gifford, 1996, p. 14). These parents are looking for an alternative. It is crucial that they choose your school not just because it is "an alternative", but because they are sufficiently aware of its program to feel that it is better for their children.

The group of parents which showed the most dissatisfaction with charter schools (4.3%) and the least likeliness to reenroll their children (10.2%) was that of those whose children had not attended school during the last year (Gifford, 1996, pp. 16–17). Some of these students may have been suspended or expelled. However, others were young children for whom the charter schools were their first school experience. It is especially important for parents of these children to visit your classrooms if your school is already in operation. In any case, a special effort should be made to explain your school's program to those parents who have not previously had school-age children.

The Goldwater survey showed that 8.4% of the parents of home-schooled children were not likely to reenroll their child in the charter school (Gifford, 1996, p. 17). At the time of initial enrollment these parents were probably quite familiar with their child and his/her academic progress, but may have been unfamiliar with larger school settings and procedures. Here again, it is essential that your staff describes your school's program in detail and discusses any transition problems which their child may face.

Your initial contact with all parents should not only provide information about your school's program, but also about parent commitment. Tell parents how charter schools differ from other public schools, how your school is governed, and what role parents play. If you use a parent contract, explain it to them and make sure they are sufficiently aware of what it entails. All parents need to know your expectations for their involvement in the school, the resources which are available to them, and their opportunities to have an input. If parents have transportation problems, speak a language other than English, or have work schedules or other family situations that make it difficult for them to participate, this is the time to work toward solutions. Families will appreciate your efforts to bring them into the school community.

A resource center

A charter school can encourage parent involvement by serving as a resource center. Among the options adopted by charter schools are parent lounges, parent workshops and classes (such as English, Spanish, citizenship, computers, parenting, family living), an early morning coffee shop, parent coffees, access to the school library, a food pantry, a health clinic, and family support services (Becker, Nakagawa, and Corwin, 1995, p. 6; "A Profile of...", 1996, pp. 38–69). These can provide families with networking opportunities and educational, social, and health services.

In selecting an option for your school, consider its potential for granting parents responsibility and empowerment. For instance, parents, with cooperation from the school staff, could be in charge of parent classes: choosing a coordinator, selecting the topics, determining the scheduling, writing announcements to send home with the children, personally inviting parents they know, and choosing and/or being class teachers.

Parents could be given responsibility for the parent lounge. With space, furniture, and funds from the school, parents could arrange the room, ensure that coffee, tea, and juice were always on hand, bring in old magazines, host and provide food for parent coffees, and contribute no-longer-used preschool and infant toys for the young children who might accompany their parents.

Just as a classroom belongs to its teachers and students, so a class for parents or a parent lounge would belong to the parents.

A contribution

It is likely that you will expect all parents to participate in parent-teacher conferences and attend the school's parent meetings. Holding parent meetings in different community sites and at different times of the week and day, arranging for a translator at teacher-family conferences, furnishing translation headsets at lectures, providing child care during meetings, and facilitating car pools are ways of promoting this commitment.

Beyond this involvement, your school should provide a variety of opportunities for parent participation. This benefits the charter school which, operating on a tight budget, can draw upon volunteer time and talents. It provides parents with the opportunity to contribute in those ways best tailored to their interests and schedules.

Offer volunteer opportunities with which you are most comfortable. For instance, some teachers may not want parent volunteers in their classrooms, while others welcome them. In the Goldwater Institute's survey of 120 Arizona charter school teachers, it found that only 35% of the teachers used parent classroom volunteers, but of these, 30% used more than three volunteers a week and four or more volunteer hours per week were contributed in 43% of these classrooms (Gifford and Keller, 1996, pp. 38–39).

Table 8 shows just some of the ways in which parents might volunteer.

The tie between parent contribution and parent ownership has been recognized by McCormack, "'We make sure that we use our parents as resources. If they have a skill, if they have something they can bring to the school in any way, we make sure that we find out what that is and we use it. And then they are in fact invested'" (Pioneer Institute for Public Policy Research, 1996, p. viii-5).

STAFF OWNERSHIP
....

When hiring staff, you looked for a fit between the applicant and the school. This fit is also important in fostering staff ownership in the school. It is revealing that of the 22% of teachers surveyed by the Goldwater Institute who did not plan to return to their charter school, one-half had chosen to teach at the school primarily because it had an opening (Gifford and Keller, 1996, p. 11). If teachers are to become owners of a school, they must be committed to its mission and willing to work extra hours and perform varied tasks to effect that mission.

Teachers will need assistance in becoming part of the school's culture. This is particularly true when the administrator and all the staff are new (Lange et al., 1996, p. 61) and also when staff in a conversion school was accustomed to teaching in a different way. The Minnesota Charter Schools Evaluation recommended that "new charter schools should plan for the socialization of members" (Lange et al., 1996, p. 64). Staff development sessions directed at acquainting staff members with each other and with the school's mission and policies as well as procedures for incorporating new staff into the school's culture will help staff members achieve school ownership.

What input will teachers have in your school? As with students and parents, teachers need to be given meaningful responsibilities and empowered to carry them out. This seems to be a strong point in charter schools where teachers generally not only have authority in their classrooms, but also a voice in such policy-making areas as grading, discipline, and school governance—and may even be school administrators.

Teachers should be made aware that their school's mission is the product of hours of deliberation and represents the consensus of the school's organizers. As noted above, teachers should have a voice in defining the school's culture, but the school's mission is a given.

Some teachers may be reluctant to share ownership with other teachers, parents and students. It is crucial that teachers know what authority they have, that areas of responsibility be clearly delineated, and that a school policy on shared responsibilities be established. Even if there is no team teaching in a classroom, the teacher will need to engage the parent as part of his/her team.

Nonteaching staff also needs to be vested with school ownership. Here again, staff members must be given the authority to carry out their designated responsibilities and to work as team members with each other and the teaching staff.

Your staff's sense of their school ownership will be reflected in staff morale and in their willingness to go the extra mile. It will affect the success of your school.

Table 8	*Parent Volunteer Options*

Arrange for speakers for student or parent meetings
Become a lunchroom or playground aide
Coach a sport
Cook food for special occasions
Coordinate parent volunteers
Design databases
Do gardening, landscaping, or maintenance work
Help on field trips
Help with vision/hearing testing
Initiate /assist with a class project
Look after the parent resource room
Make supplies for the classroom
Network with the business community
Organize car pools
Organize parent coffees
Organize/work on a used book drive for the school's library
Plan/work on school social events
Present a program in a classroom on a hobby or career
Participate in a school recycling program
Prepare students for an academic competition
Provide an internship for students
Provide professional advice
Provide repair services
Raise funds
Read to or with children in the classroom
Serve on the governing committee
Set up/ join a parent telephone network
Sponsor a new parent
Teach a parent class or workshop
Teach students how to saw, sew, knit, type, etc.
Translate school newsletters and notices
Tutor students
Volunteer in the office
Write letters to public officials
Write releases to the media

Source: Becker, Nakagawa, and Corwin, 1995, p. 6; Democratic Leadership Council, p. 12; "A Profile of...", 1996, p. 39; University of Minnesota; Weiss, 1997, p. 7.

ADMINISTRATOR / GOVERNING
BOARD OWNERSHIP
....

The success of a charter school depends to a great extent on its administrator(s) (or those responsible for administrative duties) and its governing board and the relationship between them. Throughout the charter school approval and preoperational periods you have been working through your application and your management plan to assure that responsibilities are clearly delineated and that appropriate power is vested in the responsible parties.

Mány of the responsibilities may be shared responsibilities. Further, as the school becomes operational, issues arise which, despite the best planning, have not been foreseen. Decision-making responsibility on these issues may not be clearly set forth in the school's management plan.

If these school policy and programmatic issues are to be resolved effectively and if the administrator and the governing board are to have effective ownership in the school, jurisdictional disputes must be avoided insofar as possible and, if they occur, resolved cooperatively and without rancor.

The governing board has final authority in certain areas. One of these is the hiring and firing of the administrator. The broad range of qualities necessary for administration of a charter school have been discussed in Stepping Stone 4. Once the administrator has been chosen, he/she should be allowed to fulfill the designated responsibilities without the interference of the governing board.

Linda Page, administrator of a charter school in Colorado Springs, assumed her position as the school was about to begin operation. According to Page, her efforts at leadership were undermined by board members who were often present in the school and determined to micromanage the school's operations. She was unable even to get a job description (Page with Levine, 1996, pp. 27–28). Without the empowerment to carry out what she perceived as her responsibilities, Page was deprived of her school ownership and friction ensued.

In contrast, at The EXCEL School in Durango, Colorado, a professional search, both locally and nationally, was employed to select an administrator. Telephone interviews, site interviews, and interviews at the school were part of the process. Having invested a major effort in choosing a highly competent administrator, the person chosen was given the authority to transform a "school on paper" into an operating entity, putting the curriculum in order, hiring the staff, etc. (Interview with Ballantine, 1996).

Just as the administrator must be given school ownership by the governing board, so the administrator must be willing to share ownership with his/her staff. Once capable staff members have been chosen, the administrator must be a leader, but not a micromanager.

Likewise, it is crucial to give ownership to your governing board. Being a charter school board member requires considerable know-how, and training for governing board members should be a high priority (Fitzgerald, 1995, p. 26; Nathan, 1996, p. 147). Your governing board must be responsive to its constituents. It will exercise major responsibilities and be vested with final authority in specified areas. Even though your board adopts a "hands-off" policy, you will find that it may perform additional supportive services to the school. For instance, Ballantine, a board member, mentioned that as her school had discovered that it needed to provide more of a challenge for its higher-end students, she was investigating programs at two other charter schools (Interview, 1996).

Governing board members, like the others involved with your school, need to feel that their contributions are meaningful and rewarding. The extent of satisfaction which they experience in their school ownership will impact their commitment and their enthusiasm.

Stepping Stone 8

....

Establish Communication Procedures and Make Effective Communication a Continuing Priority

Effective communication is a critical element in the success of any organization. For a charter school, which is both school and business, it is especially crucial that there be effective communication within the school and with each of its constituencies. "Lack of familiarity", not only among administrators, staff, and parents, but also with the schools themselves, presents a challenge (Lange et al., 1996, p. 61). To be effective, communication should be two-way and both structured and informal.

INTRA-SCHOOL COMMUNICATION
....

When you were on the organizing committee, your communications with other committee members were probably fairly casual. Even though your committee and subcommittee meetings followed agendas, the overall atmosphere was more than likely an informal one.

It is important that you maintain this informality—that all staff members and the administrator freely communicate in the halls, around the water cooler, and in on-the-spot meetings to exchange information, resolve immediate problems, air frustrations, and just brainstorm someone's latest idea. Likewise, in school meetings it is important that there be a comfortable atmosphere in which there is an easy give-and-take and in which even the more reticent staff members participate.

However, now that you have an operating school in which staff members are carrying out their responsibilities in different parts of the building (or out of the building) and where individual schedules often preclude immediate communication, it is important that you establish communication procedures and forms.

Your school will develop its own forms and procedures. In each case, the forms and procedures should be developed through or with the concurrence of those involved and should be reevaluated on a yearly or other basis.

Among the forms which your school may develop are:

- visitor sign-in,
- student attendance,
- staff check-in and check-out,
- staff-parent contacts,
- staff leave requests,
- suspected child abuse,
- injury and behavior incidents,
- test results,
- teacher referral of children with possible special education needs,
- special education observations,
- the results of support staff interventions, and/or
- conflict resolution.

Procedures should be written to accompany each of these forms as well as for other situations.

Communicating by written memorandums has several advantages. Memorandums can lessen the need for meetings, save time otherwise spent in telling the information to several persons, assure that each person gets the same information, allow each person to read the information at a convenient time, and provide a record of what has been presented.

There needs to be continuing communication among the staff, whether between team teachers or between classroom teachers and support staff. The administrator needs to learn of staff members' needs and concerns. The regular scheduling of individual supervision sessions can help meet this need, especially if it is a time for open and confidential dialogue. Staff input in the school should come not only through those staff members who are on the governing board, but also through committees of staff members which are responsible for such areas as evaluation tools and staff development. Major decisions on individual children should be made by all those working with the child after each has communicated his/her observations. Staff meetings, both those regularly scheduled and those which are more impromptu, are also effective means of promoting communication.

SCHOOL–PARENT COMMUNICATION

Your staff will be communicating with parents by sending home such items as incident reports; notices of IEP meetings; information on classroom routine, policies and plans; requests for specific items or volunteers; notices of testing (including permission slips); a school calendar; school newsletters; and examples of the child's work. Materials should be written in the family's primary language or a language in which it is proficient. Responsibility for contacting parents in different situations should be delineated among the family coordinator, the teacher, the counselor, etc.

Likewise, procedures should be developed for the sharing of individual test results.

School–parent communication is a two-way process. Staff members need to communicate often with parents. Drop-off and pick-up times as well as times when the parent visits the classroom or volunteers on field trips are ideal occasions for informal communication. However, there are those parents whose children ride the bus and who are not available for classroom volunteering. Communicating by written notes and by telephone calls can help build a teacher-parent team that can share information on the child's progress and difficulties, develop individualized strategies for dealing with problems, and rejoice together at each accomplishment.

Likewise, parents can communicate with teachers by writing notes, telephoning, and sending papers or drawings done at home. Information on their child's health, activities, and homework problems will also key the teacher in to the child's progress and needs.

Parent meetings provide opportunities for parents and staff to touch base. Parent–teacher and parent–teacher–student conferences, whether for reporting progress, dealing with behavior problems, or writing IEP's, should be an opportunity for all involved to share their concerns, opinions, and goals.

SCHOOL–COMMUNITY COMMUNICATION

You have already seen how community support contributed to your charter's approval. School–community communication should continue to be a priority. Never forget that you are a public school with public responsibilities and public accountability. Legally, your governing board meetings must be open. The results of your student evaluations should also be open to the public so that prospective parents can make informed school choices.

A positive school image will go far towards quieting the naysayers who are ready to fault your operations, and your community's support will be invaluable at charter renewal time. In addition, a strong school marketing program will greatly facilitate your fund-raising.

Select someone to handle your marketing efforts. It may be your administrator, a staff member, or a governing board member or perhaps you can secure the pro bono services of a public relations firm.

Pay special attention to your surrounding community, your neighborhood. Get to know your neighbors and consider recruiting at least one of them for your governing board. Hold an open house, send out notices of school events, and take seriously any complaints. You may wish to hold meetings at which neighbors discuss their concerns, e.g., traffic problems, the behavior of your students off campus. If needed, set up a joint school-neighborhood committee to resolve pressing issues.

Establish a personal relationship with the media. Invite them as well as city officials, legislators, and business leaders to visit your school. Keep the media informed of school activities and projects. You may even want your students to write news releases (as well as to speak or perform for community groups). Display copies of favorable articles in your visitor area and consider preparing a media publicity packet (Horowitz, 1996, p. 23).

SCHOOL–SPONSORING AGENCY COMMUNICATION

You will be required to communicate to your sponsoring agency certain particulars of your operation. Check as to what reporting is required. For instance, in Massachusetts where charter schools are chartered by the state board of education, each school must submit an annual report, an enrollment report, other reports required by public school law and regulations, its code of conduct, notification of any change in circumstances significantly impacting the school, and additional information which the board might require (Commonwealth of Massachusetts, Department of Education, 1997c, pp. 17-18).

Besides these required communications, you will want to establish and maintain a strong working relationship with your sponsoring agency. Mark Levine, a Colorado charter school administrator, advises charter schools to "try to have your relations with your chartering district as clarified, as spelled out, as possible." To do so, he suggests that, in addition to the "broad outline" of the charter agreement, each school and its sponsoring district enter into an "operating contract" that is more directed towards the school's daily operations (Interview, 1996).

A major responsibility of your administrator should be keeping the lines of communication open between your school and the school superintendent or other officials in your sponsoring agency. For instance, Ray Rodriguez of Colorado's Community Prep School meets monthly with his district's administration to go over academic issues and problems (Interview, 1997).

Spend time locating those persons in your sponsoring agency's administrative staff who can provide the technical assistance you will need in such areas as special education or purchasing procedures. Designate those of your staff members who are responsible for these areas as your school's contacts with these "experts". Encourage them to establish personal relationships with their sponsoring agency counterparts, meeting them personally and maintaining telephone contact. This will not only be a means of gaining useful information, but also of giving your sponsoring agency the message that you value its input.

If your sponsoring agency is not your school district, determine in which areas you wish to receive school district services, e.g., transportation, and establish and maintain your contacts. Your sponsoring agency should be able to provide you with information as to the relationship of charter schools and their local school districts in your state.

Stepping Stone 9

Institute a Management System That Is Role-Specific, Time-Efficient, People-Friendly, and Change-Responsive

"At charter schools, every policy, every position, everything the school does for the first time must be created. So decisions, both small and large, need to be made frequently and should be made efficiently" (Weiss, 1997, p. 11). Indeed, as Weiss has pointed out, the newness of charter schools makes their administration an extraordinarily difficult challenge. On the other hand, it permits schools to be innovative in coming up with the management systems best suited for their educational missions. Creation of these systems is a continuing process. Determine the goals which you want for your particular management system. This stepping stone suggests that it be role-specific, time-efficient, people-friendly, and change-responsive.

ROLE-SPECIFIC
....

In order to be role-specific your school must clearly designate responsibility for all of the tasks it is to perform and ensure that the entire staff is aware both of who is in charge and to whom they are accountable. What are the tasks?

First, determine those areas in which you are legally responsible. Stepping Stones 4 and 5 looked at the legal issues which you needed to address in your application and during your start-up period, but now that your school is in business, there are more areas in which your school's operations must be circumspect. Table 9 lists some of them. Go over these and other relevant areas with your attorney and those experienced in business and school operating procedures. Become sufficiently conversant with the requirements that you will be able to comply with them in your daily operations. Then, determine what reports are required.

There are, of course, countless other tasks which your school must perform. Among these are the establishment of communications procedures, which were discussed in the preceding stepping stone. Playground and lunchroom supervision, tending to children who become ill or injured, keeping track of supply room needs, and scheduling the school's van are just a few of the others.

Don't become so focused on the myriad of tasks that must be performed that you overlook your responsibility to your educational program. Working on the development of curriculum and assessment measures and giving support to staff are important areas which should be covered by your management system.

It cannot be said too often that for each task responsibility should be assigned and accountability established. Once you have determined responsibilities, as pointed out in Stepping Stone 7, you will need to empower those assigned to perform them. The combination of capable, conscientious staff members, staff ownership, and specific, clearly communicated and accepted role designation should go far towards fostering a productive working community.

Table 9	*Areas of Legal Concern*

Bidding/purchasing procedures
Bylaw violations
Charter statute violations
Charter violations
Child abuse
Civil rights
Conflicts of interest, including nepotism
Contract violations
Drug, alcohol, and tobacco usage
Embezzlement
Emergency procedures
Employee hiring and firing
Employment practices
Facility permits
Federal program requirements
Fiscal procedures
Grant requirements
Liability
Medication procedures
Nonsectarian policies, including censorship
Open meetings, including proper notification
Parent permission
Parent rights
Privacy
Public records
School district requirements
Special education
Standards of conduct
State regulations
Student discipline policies
Taxes
Teacher mentoring requirements
Test score manipulation
Vehicle and driver requirements
Zoning restrictions

TIME-EFFICIENT

••••••••••••••••••••••••

Like any business, charter schools need to be time efficient. In fact, with the many, often novel, tasks which staff members must perform and with the many different roles which each of them must play, the need to plan ahead and to be efficient is an especially pressing one.

From the days of developing your application you have kept a master calendar. The need for such a calendar is even greater now. Mark down the dates on which particular requirements must be met and reports must be completed. Also, note on the calendar dates important to the school's operation, including those of parent meetings, staff development sessions, parent conferences, governing board meetings, staff meetings, pupil count day, and field trips. For each of these dates determine and add to the calendar the dates of meetings, preliminary reports, etc. which should precede these due dates. For instance, you may want to schedule a meeting at which some of the staff plan the parent meeting, a date by which a notice should be sent home to parents on the importance of having their children present on the pupil count day, and dates on which parents should be called to schedule their individual conferences.

Encourage individual staff members to develop their own work calendars. For example, the person responsible for your students with IEP's will need to do a great amount of scheduling. For each child he/she will need to write down the dates of thirty day reviews; perhaps quarterly reviews; annual reviews; intervention times; times for consultation with the classroom teacher; times for contacting parents; times for testing not only by the special education teacher but by the occupational therapist, the speech therapist, etc.; a date at which those familiar with the child can share observations prior to the staffing meeting; the parent staffing notification deadline date; and the staffing date.

Stepping Stone 8 pointed out the advantages of communicating by written memorandums. Meetings will also be essential to your school, but it hardly has to be pointed out that they can be very time-consuming. Try to keep meetings to a minimum.

Plan for meeting times when setting up your school's weekly schedule. Create times when team teachers will be free for planning and when both teachers and their support staff will have the same free periods so that they may share observations and develop strategies. Schedule times during which the whole staff may participate in staff development sessions, staff meetings, and, especially important in schools which are developing their own curriculum or assessment tools, staff planning sessions. Make it easier for individual staff members to arrange on-the-spot meetings by having staff members post and circulate their weekly work calendars.

For essential meetings include all those involved. In some cases those who will not attend should submit a written report summarizing their observations, experiences, and/or opinions.

At the meeting give time for each person to express his/her views. Encourage brainstorming, but stick to the point. Your meeting moderator should summarize what has been decided so that any omissions or misunderstandings can be immediately detected. A copy of the meeting's minutes or summary should be sent to each person concerned.

Finally, include free time for the unexpected on both the master and the individual calendars.

PEOPLE-FRIENDLY

For maximum effectiveness, your management system must be not only efficient, but also people-friendly. This can be achieved in part by assuring administrator and staff ownership, by planning ahead, and by communicating to all members of the staff what is going on and the role they will play.

So far charter school teachers are, for the most part, experiencing satisfaction in their jobs (Lange, 1996, p. 16; Weiss, 1997, p. i). However, a thundercloud looms on the horizon. It represents the dangers of work overload, of the buildup of fatigue, stress, and ultimately poor morale that can result from sustained extra-hour effort. According to Weiss, "Staff burn-out is a major concern" (1997, p. 13).

Whether you are a new or an existing charter school, this problem cannot be ignored. Lange et al. pointed to the problems of expecting staff "to efficiently develop curriculum at the same time they provide instruction" (p. xviii) and to the students who "are always there" (1996, p. xiv). Somehow, time must be included in the schedule to allow staff members to fulfill the additional duties which they perform in a charter school. There is no easy answer to this problem. This is an area in which it will be helpful for you to seek technical assistance, to network with other charter schools, and to brainstorm solutions. It is one of the biggest obstacles you will face—but then, by now you are used to surmounting obstacles.

CHANGE-RESPONSIVE

"Many Minnesota charter schools are coping with the widely held assumption that planning and implementation are discrete and separable stages in the process of major change. These changes require evolutionary planning, in which action and development are deliberately intertwined over a relatively long period of time" (Lange et al., 1996, p. xvii). You spent hours, days, and weeks planning during the application and preoperational periods. Once school started, you were ready to implement your plans. You have so many tasks to perform just to operate your school that you hesitate to take time out for planning. But, as pointed out above, planning is part of the action.

Take time to plan ahead, not just for the next year but for the long term. Set goals and objectives and establish timelines.

Your management plan must embrace your planning and the implementation of those changes which planning produces. In fact, your management plan itself must be responsive to change. Charter schools have rejected the bureaucracy of public school and school district administration. Don't create your own bureaucracy. Incorporate flexibility not only into your thinking, but also into your management plan.

Stepping Stone 10

....

Actively Pursue New Funding
Sources and Arrangements

Whether you are a budding charter applicant, in your preoperational period, in your first year of operation, or an established charter school, the time to pursue new funding sources and arrangements is now. Regardless of the extent to which your operational funding matches those of neighboring public schools and whether or not you have a rent-free facility requiring no renovation, you will probably need outside funding and/or innovative cost-saving arrangements to succeed financially. As Meera Mani, first administrator of Denver's Clayton Charter School, stated, "Schools can't operate on PPOR [per pupil operating revenue]" (Interview, 1996).

FUNDING SOURCES

....

Check on possible fund-raising restrictions in your state. Of the sixteen charter schools covered in Minnesota's charter school evaluation, 69% received technical assistance, half received monetary support, half also received in-kind support, and 19% received staff training during their planning period (Lange et al., 1996, p. xii). However, charter schools in that state are faced with funding restrictions after the planning/start-up periods (pp. 52-53).

Table 10 gives just a few examples of the companies, organizations, foundations, institutions, and governmental units which have supported charter schools. Look at it closely, not so much to note the specific names listed, but to examine the types of support which you can pursue.

Some of these organizations are the forces behind the establishment of charter schools and are integrally related to the schools' operations. The City of Colorado Springs not only employs the staff of the Community Prep School, but also provides the site in a city building and offers students the opportunity to draw upon the wide range of resources and occupational expertise represented in the city government (Interview with Rodriguez, 1997). Middlesex Community College in Lowell, Massachusetts provides an on-campus site for the Lowell Middlesex Academy, makes all its facilities available to its students, and allows students to enroll in its classes (Pioneer Institute..., APP-B, 1996).

If you are a charter applicant, examine the option of securing such a close relationship with an existing organization. Even if your school will be more autonomous, try to find a site which will provide, as a bonus, access to the in-kind services which can benefit your program, both educationally and financially.

Look at the variety of businesses listed in Table 10. The Amoco Foundation gave the EXCEL Academy in Arvada, Colorado two $500 grants because of the volunteer work which two Amoco employees had done at the school ("Excel Academy To Receive Grant", 1996). The Durango Foundation for Educational Excellence gave a $6,000 grant to The EXCEL School in that Colorado city for its administrator search and has continued to support the school through small grants for field trips (Interview with Ballantine, 1996). Look for grants and in-kind assistance from both national and local organizations.

Search for potential participant foundations in your library and on the Internet and compile a list of prospective

Table 10
Examples of Companies, Organizations, Foundations, Institutions, and Governmental Units Which Have Partnered with/Awarded Grants to Charter Schools

Amoco Foundation
Apple Computer
Archdiocese of Boston Hispanic Youth Leadership Program
Black Men of Greater Springfield
Boston Harbor Project Training Program
Boston Symphony
Cape Cod National Seashore
Castle Hill Center for the Arts
City of Colorado Springs
County of San Diego
Durango Foundation for Educational Excellence
Hewlett Packard
Hull Council for Business & Cultural Development
James Baldwin Scholars Program
Lower Merrimack Valley Regional Employment Board
Middlesex Community College
National Gardening Association
Northern States Power Co.
Pacific Oaks College
Piton Foundation
Round Valley Adopt-a-Watershed Project
Solano County Office of Education
Springfield YMCA
Teamsters Union
U.S. Navy Helicopter Squadron 41
U.S. West
University of California at Berkeley
University of Southern Colorado
Wellfleet Massachusetts Audubon Wildlife Sanctuary
Wells Fargo Bank
World Affairs Council

Source: Finn, Manno, and Bierlein, 1996, p. 19; Interviews with Ballantine, Mani, and Rodriguez; Mulholland and Bierlein, 1995, p. 39: Nathan, 1996, p. 28; Pioneer Institute for Public Policy Research, 1996, APP-B; A Profile of California's Charter Schools..., 1996, pp. 2-85.

companies in your community. Don't forget labor unions and community organizations such as the YMCA and museums. Have you ever heard of U.S. Navy Helicopter Squadron 41, the Wellfleet Massachusetts Audubon Wildlife Sanctuary, or the James Baldwin Scholars Program? Charter schools in Chula Vista, California and in Orleans and Springfield, Massachusetts had and enlisted them as school partners (Pioneer Institute..., 1996, APP-B; A Profile of..., 1996, p. 85). This is an area in which you can and should exercise your initiative.

The first year progress report of the National Study of Charter Schools pointed out, "Most charter schools are eligible for Title I funding, but some may not be aware of eligibility procedures" (RPP International and University of Minnesota, 1997, p. 25). Don't overlook the federal Public Charter Schools, Title I, Title VI, Safe and Drug-Free Schools, and Dwight D. Eisenhower Professional Development Program grants or federal special education and Child Nutrition funds. One source of information is the *Guide to the U.S. Department of Education Programs* (U.S. Department of Education, 1997). Also, determine the state funding for which you are eligible.

Decide which persons will be primarily responsible for fund-raising. Your administrator and/or designated board members might assume this responsibility. Arrange for training in grant writing. Determine what kind of assistance you are seeking: loans, technical assistance, monetary grants, donations of equipment or facilities, pro bono services, staff training, memberships or reduced admissions, work internships.

Gregory Roberts, executive director of Summerbridge National Office in San Francisco, suggested at the 1997 CANEC conference that you first involve a prospect's employees as school volunteers [as did the EXCEL Academy]. Your proposal should specify exactly what you are seeking and should include a means of evaluating the effects of the assistance. You should also provide your partners with relevant updates (*Marketing and Fundraising*, 1997). Other tips provided at the same conference by Kevin Sved, cofounder and codirector of The Accelerated School in Los Angeles, included stressing the benefits to the prospective partner and showing how the plan will be implemented (*Marketing and Fundraising*, 1997).

Finally, don't be so busy looking for outside funding sources that you overlook fund-raising possibilities at your school. For what services can you charge fees? Can you provide after-school day care or rent out your facility during off-hours for meetings? In San Fernando, California the Vaughn Next Century Learning Center Charter School is planning a computer repair shop, a uniform outlet, and a bookstore which even serves coffee (Chan, 1997). What innovative fund-raising strategies can you come up with?

FUNDING ARRANGEMENTS

In developing your charter application you investigated different cost-saving arrangements. Continue to do so. Various options have been discussed in Stepping Stone 4. Look especially at the areas of site support, food services, and recreation. For instance, contracting for local groundskeeping services saved money for Palm Desert, California's Washington Charter School as well as cutting down on school-hour noise (A Profile of..., 1996, p. 71).

In deciding upon your funding arrangements, keep in mind the educational, as well as the financial, implications for your school.

Stepping Stone 11

....

Base Decisions at Every Level on the Criterion: "This School Is for the Students."

This stepping stone could have been placed almost anywhere on the path to creating and running a charter school.

However, when your school was being organized, you were well aware that it was being set up for the students. Although you spent countless hours making the major and minor decisions involved in preparing your organizational plan, it is a good bet that most of you preferred working on your educational program: defining your mission and outcomes and developing the curriculum and assessment tools which would help your students succeed.

Then, as you prepared your school for opening and greeted the arriving students, you were caught up with the excitement of your new program and with effecting the promises it held for student success.

Now, as this stage has passed, you may well be feeling the frustrations of coping with seemingly endless and unexpected problems, the weariness resulting from long working hours, the personality conflicts which are no longer masked by enthusiasm, and the enormous pressures from your community and sponsoring agency to prove that you can succeed as a charter school. This is the time to remember that your school was founded to serve the students and that they should be the focal point of all your decisions.

Table 11
Measures of School (= Student) Success

Students
    Academic performance
    Attendance
    College acceptance
    Dropouts
    Involvement
    Meeting of individual needs
    Progress (all domains)
    Satisfaction
    Suspension/expulsion
    Test scores
    Turnover
    Voice in school

Parents
    Involvement
    Satisfaction
    Voice in school

Staff /administrator
    Commitment
    Enthusiasm
    Morale
    Satisfaction
    Turnover
    Voice in school

Governing board
    Civility
    Efficiency
    Enthusiasm
    Support
    Voice of all constituencies

School
    Accreditation
    Expansion in number of grades
    Expansion in number of students
    Financial viability

Sponsoring agency
    Support

Community
    Financial support
    Reputation of school
    Waiting list

MEASURES OF SUCCESS

Are you a successful school? How can you measure your success? First, of course, are you fulfilling the goals set forth in your mission statement? Just as your school's vision differs from those of other schools, so also the measures of how you will achieve it will be unique to your school.

There are, however, more common measures of charter school success. Some of them are listed in Table 11.

The title of Table 11 is not a misnomer. The true success of your school will come only when your students are successful. You can achieve some modicum of success while focusing on a good public image, fund-raising, expansion, and/or the fulfillment of personal goals, but real success will come only when you make your students your priority.

STUDENTS

To make decisions based on the welfare of your students, it makes sense to look at your students. You have come up with student assessment tools. How successful are your students when measured by these tools?

If the answer is "Not very" or "There are widespread discrepancies", first reexamine your educational program. Are the objectives which you set the ones you really want? Is your curriculum effective in achieving these objectives? Will you need to change it, adapt it to your student population, or supplement it? Is your instructional approach effective? Does it jibe with the curriculum you have selected? Finally, do the assessment tools you have selected really measure student progress in meeting the established objectives? In fact, the process of reexamining your educational program should be a continuing one, regardless of the success of your students on the assessment measures. There is always room for improvement.

Second, look at individual student results. Especially look at those students who are doing well and those who are not. It may seem unnecessary to look at students who excel, but they may provide insights that will help you with other students. Did they enter your school performing at a high level? Do they all learn in the same manner, e.g., verbally, experientially? Do they have strong parent support? Are they clustered with particular teachers? Do they succeed because everyone expects them to?

Adapting your program to different learning styles, higher expectations, assisting parents in helping at home, transferring students to other teachers, and breaking up groups who reinforce each other's poor behavior are some of the strategies which may help those students who are not doing well. Look at each student individually. Are there previously undetected special education needs or signs of abuse? Are there problems at home: a new sibling, a divorce? Is the child having problems socially?

Regardless of how the student is doing, communicate with the parent and student through conferences. Get their input and take it seriously. When there are problems, brainstorm not only with the parent, but also with all the staff members involved with the child. How can you adapt your teaching approach with this child? What additional help can you give—and what should the student do in return? Look back at the section in Stepping Stone 7 on student ownership.

Is this the best school for this particular child? In discussing this sensitive issue with parents, make sure that the student's welfare (not your own) is the criterion. It would be so much easier for you if a troublemaker is removed from your class. It would boost the school's test scores if children with academic problems leave. But is this what your school was set up to accomplish?

Try everything you can to improve the success of even the most difficult student. Realistically balance the needs of this student and of the other children in the class. Are the other students being unfairly affected by the disruption of the class-room or can they be involved as part of the solution? It is likely that your charter school has smaller classes and gives more personal attention than other schools the student has attended or may attend. Your school may be the student's best hope—and, if you can pull it off, this child will be your biggest success.

In evaluating your school's focus on its students, deter-mine their satisfaction. Is their attendance high, are they happy at your school, does each one experience the pride of success, do they have ownership? Ask your students what they like and don't like. You don't have to adopt their sug-gestions, but do consider them objectively.

PARENTS

Student success is often mirrored in the satisfaction level of their parents. The positive or negative feedback which they give you, their decisions to enroll younger siblings or to transfer their child to a different school are means by which they tell you whether or not you are making the right deci-sions for their child. To be sure, there are parents who are never satisfied, but by and large the degree of parent satisfac-tion depends on the success of their children.

At charter schools parents are, or should be, given the opportunity to become involved in the school and to have a voice on the governing board. If, from the beginning, parents have been committed to your school's mission, they will be responsible advocates for your school's students, and their opinions should be taken seriously.

STAFF/ADMINISTRATOR

Does the overriding criterion of doing what's best for your students mean that the needs of your staff and administrator are of secondary importance? Absolutely not. If the adults at your school are not happy, it is unlikely that your students will be. If there is excessive turnover among your school's personnel, your students cannot help but be affected.

Staff and administrator ownership were discussed in Stepping Stone 7 and the need to avoid work overload was stressed in Stepping Stone 9. Your school's environment, addressed in Stepping Stone 6, is a working as well as a learning environment. The needs of your staff and administrator are enmeshed with those of your students. Whatever you can do to increase their morale and commitment will enhance student success.

GOVERNING BOARD

It should go without saying that contention within the governing board and between the governing board and the administrator or with the sponsoring agency and/or school district will not be in the best interests of either the school or its students. Governing board members will have to work hard to further the school's, not their own, agenda, to admit and learn from mistakes, and to be solution-seekers. Honest differences of opinion are to be honored and welcomed, but if decision-making has become a problem, seek assistance from those trained in governing board procedures and decision-making.

POLICY DECISIONS
•••••••••••••••••••••••••••••••

Just as decisions regarding individual students should be based on what is best for that student, so also more general policy decisions should be based on the same criterion. Regardless of whether these decisions are made by the administrator, school committees, individual staff members, or the governing board, don't lose sight of the students. Should your school expand to more grade levels? This would bring more revenue into the school, but would your facilities be too cramped for your enlarged school population? Would a sudden increase in enrollment without adequate preparation impact negatively the students you are currently serving? Is it better to spend funds on improving your school's appearance or on additional staff? Should your school make cuts in staff or services that will adversely affect your students in the short run, but will assure that the school will have the financial resources to serve them next year? Will the decision you are making compromise your school's mission?

Let your discussions and debates focus on what is best for the students. After all, they're who the school is for.

Stepping Stone 12

....

Anticipate That Each Day Will Be Different: New Travelers, New Terrain, New Sunrises, and New Sunsets

You are into your first year. Your full staff is on board, your parents have become involved, your teachers and students are engrossed in various learning activities, your management system is in place, and your governing board has held its first meetings. Together you have mastered the hurdles of school start-up. Your school is in operation. You have made it a reality.

You are all set—right? Wrong. You are never all set. Each year, each month, each day, even each hour will offer something new. Perhaps anticipated, perhaps unexpected; perhaps major, perhaps minor; perhaps an obstacle, perhaps a breakthrough; perhaps a bad break, perhaps a windfall—there is always something that comes up. You are never all set. You are still on your journey.

NEW TRAVELERS
....

Even within each school year you will find that you have new travelers on your charter school journey. Students come and go. The new student does not just fill in the last student's slot. Each one is different. The student may have an IEP or be limited in his/her English proficiency, and arrangements will have to be made for meeting these needs. Further, whenever any child leaves or joins a class, there are new opportunities and challenges for the staff as well as changes in classroom dynamics. Your classroom will not be the same. In fact, one child can change your whole classroom environment, for better or for worse. Each new student brings with him/her a new family. There are different parents or other family members to be involved or not involved in your parent group or volunteer activities, to offer suggestions or criticism, to be part of your school community.

Even if your staff turnover is limited, you may well have new volunteers, interns, and/or part-time support staff in your classroom, all requiring input from your staff and introducing their own individual styles. When new staff does come on board, there will be new dynamics and challenges, both within classroom teaching teams and in overall staff interactions—and your students will have to make adjustments.

Changes are more marked at the beginning of each school year. There may be a number of new staff members, and staff socialization will be a priority. Mentoring and staff development sessions can help your new staff become familiar with and immersed in your school's culture.

Each class has its own personality and whether or not your school uses single- or multi-age groupings, the departure of your graduating students and the entering of a new group of younger students will make a difference in your school's environment. Further, teachers will need to begin each year orienting a new class and learning how to respond to the individual needs of each child.

With each year the group of parents will change and perhaps also its "personality". Mani mentioned that at Clayton Charter School there was an increase in family support and a "more academically-focused" parent group (Interview, 1996).

The composition of your governing board will also change as members move away, their terms expire, or their children leave the school. Needless to say, changes in governing board membership can significantly affect both the policies it makes and its decision-making process.

NEW TERRAIN
....

Just as your band of travelers changes, so also does the terrain you will be traversing. The first year you will be faced with all the problems of newness: of getting the school ready for start-up, of discovering areas you overlooked, of making a myriad of policy decisions, of doing everything for the first time.

Sandra Elliott, administrator of the Roosevelt-Edison Charter School in Colorado Springs, pointed out that there can be an "implementation dip" during the first year, a "normal downslide" in which the staff can be overwhelmed by the "enormity of the whole thing" with no experience to draw upon (Interview, 1996). When the initial enthusiasm fades, when the working hours mount, and when teaching results are not immediately apparent, the school may have to draw upon its resources to cross some rocky terrain.

The later years will in some ways be easier. Everything is not completely new. There can be more of a long-term perspective, less concentrating on where next to place your foot, and more attending to the vista. Everything does not have to be accomplished at once (Weiss, 1997, pp. 18–19). Further, the pressures of meeting the demands of your start-up budget will be behind you.

There may, however, be new obstacles in your path. School expansion, often encompassing the addition of new grade levels, will present demands in developing curriculum, hiring staff, and managing a larger-sized school. Increased enrollment, inability to renew a lease, or other situations may require relocation. Especially if you have had early problems, your school's operations may be under increased public scrutiny. New laws and regulations may have a positive or negative effect on your school's operations. Perhaps a new alternative school or an improved neighborhood school will drain your potential student pool. Then, inevitably, as you approach the ending date of your charter's term, the charter renewal process will loom on your horizon.

Finally, there will be changes in the persons whom you meet on your journey: the new or departing personnel within your school district and/or your sponsoring agency who provide services to your school or determine overall policy. You will not only have to establish new contacts and relationships, but in some cases a new district superintendent or new board members may affect the difficulty or ease of your journey. They too are part of the terrain.

NEW SUNRISES

Each day you will face a different sunrise. Start out by planning the day's tasks. They will be determined in part by the changes in your group of travelers and in the upcoming terrain. As you plan, you will recognize that even the best laid plans will be altered or waylaid by the day's unforeseen crises—so include time for the unexpected.

The new day will require not only planning, but forward progress. Look back at your earlier experiences. Evaluate them, make the necessary changes, determine your new emphases. For instance, Mani pointed to her school's new emphases on evaluation and intensive staff training (Interview 1996). Don't be complacent. Remember that innovation was a cornerstone of your school and should remain so. Take time to "critique, move ahead" (Interview with Brown, 1997).

If you need to find a new site, look back at Stepping Stone 4 and/or review your earlier experiences. This time you will have to make plans also for moving your school to a new location with all that entails in terms of accessibility to your current population, transportation needs, and, of course, budgetary demands.

Begin your preparation for charter renewal from your school's outset by focusing on your goals, working towards financial solvency, and keeping extensive records. Charter school renewal guidelines in School District R-1 in Colorado require submittal of a report tying progress towards the goals spelled out in the initial application and contract, a financial statement, and compliance with relevant laws and standards of fiscal management (Jefferson County…, 1996). Determine the requirements in your state, including the availability of an appeals process. Again, marshal community support and work towards getting your charter renewed for the longest possible term.

NEW SUNSETS

As sunset approaches and you prepare to bed for the night, the trials you have just experienced and the problems you will face the next day may well occupy your thoughts. But, this is the time to appreciate the sunset, to reflect on what you have done, to relax and to enjoy. As Nathan has urged, "Finally, take time to celebrate accomplishments" (1996, p. 164).

Each new day will always be a commencement, but each passing day can also be a graduation. Hold planned and impromptu celebrations, including your staff, your parents, your students, and/or whomever else you want to include. Celebrate the end of each year, your charter renewal, your selection as an exemplary school, but also celebrate improved pupil performance, the receipt of a financial grant, the completion of a student project, parent participation, a great staff, great students, a great school.

Pause often in your journey to look back on the path you have traveled, to see how far you have come. You have followed and are following the stepping stones to become and continue as a successful charter school. In the process you are laying new stepping stones for others to follow. You are no longer just a pioneer in the charter school movement. You have become a charter school guide.

Appendix A

··

Glossary

A

Accelerated Schools Project—program in which schools adopt the Accelerated Schools' goal of powerful learning, its three philosophical principles, and its process for transforming their schools

ACS—average cost per student

ADA—average daily attendance

Administrator—person or persons designated by the governing board to manage a charter school's operations

AFT—American Federation of Teachers

Alternative school—public school offering an educational program differing from that offered in its district's other public schools

Alternative Public Schools LLC—for-profit company that provides school management services including a customized curriculum

American Federation of Teachers—teachers' labor union

Americans with Disabilities Act—federal statute which prohibits discrimination against persons with disabilities and requires accommodations to ensure that discrimination does not occur in such areas as public access to facilities and services, transportation, and communication

ASL—American Sign Language

Assessment—measurement of student attainment

Atlas Communities Project—educational design that features establishment of a pre-K–12 pathway incorporating basic skills and thinking skills, the use of an integrated curriculum, active inquiry, and authentic assessment

At-risk student—student who is less likely to succeed in a typical school environment

Audrey Cohen College System of Education—school design in which K–12 students develop and effect a program embracing different subjects and skills to achieve each semester's developmentally-appropriate, community-focused purpose

Authentic assessment—performance assessment

Autonomy—legal status of a charter school and extent to which it controls the provision of services which are usually provided by a school district

B

Board of trustees—governing board

C

CANEC—California Network of Educational Charters

Cap—limit on the number of charter schools allowed

Categorical program—federal or state program providing funding for a specific purpose, e.g., special education, Title I

CATO—schools in California that serve home school parents and students

Chapter 1—now Title I, ESEA

Chapter 2—now Title VI, ESEA

Character education—approach which promotes the development of core ethical values and of civil and caring school communities

Charter—contract entered into by a public sponsoring agency and school organizers which establishes a charter school and grants it rights and privileges

Charter school—public school of choice which is authorized by state statute and which is established by and operates under the terms of a charter granted to school organizers by a public sponsoring agency to whom the school is thereafter accountable

Child Nutrition—federal National School Lunch, School Breakfast, and Special Milk programs for eligible low- and moderate-income students

Coalition of Essential Schools—learning community of schools subscribing to Theodore R. Sizer's nine common principles, including students as workers and mastery of a limited number of essentials

COLA—cost of living adjustment

Community school—charter school (in Ohio)

CO-NECT Schools—school design that features multi-grade clusters, interdisciplinary projects, performance standards and assessments, and the use of technology

Conversion charter school—school that was originally a public or private school

Core Knowledge Sequence—curriculum detailing the specific knowledge to be taught in grades K through 6 in American and world civilization, geography, language arts, math, music, science, and visual arts

Criterion-referenced test—test in which a student's scores measure the extent to which his/her performance meets established performance standards

D

D.A.R.E.—Drug Abuse Resistance Education Program

Demographics—characteristics of the geographical area and/or the population served

Different Ways of Knowing (DWoK)—curriculum from the Galef Institute that features interdisciplinary, experiential, thematic learning

Distance learning—learning in which students learn off-site through the Internet, textbooks, radio and television, audio and video cassettes, etc.

Dwight D. Eisenhower Professional Development Program—federal program supporting professional development in mathematics, science, and other core academic subjects that will facilitate student attainment of state standards; Title II, ESEA

E

Edison Project—private endeavor in which the Edison Project assumes responsibility for running partnership schools whose programs feature an extended school day and year, a computer in each student's home, and an emphasis on academics and parent involvement

Efficacy—educational approach that embodies the concept of confidence promoting effort which in turn promotes development that leads to the preparation of children for the 21st century

Elementary and Secondary Education Act of 1965—federal statute reauthorized by the Improving America's School Act of 1994

Elitist school—school that restricts admission to those students most likely to succeed

ESEA—Elementary and Secondary Education Act

ESL—English as a second language

Exit outcome—objective which students are expected to attain before graduating

Expeditionary Learning Outward Bound—K–12 school design in which students learn through pursuing multidisciplinary, hands-on learning expeditions involving fieldwork and service

Experiential learning—learning through a student's active, meaningful interaction with his/her environment

F

Focus school—alternative school

Food count—number of meals served

Foxfire—approach in which students use cultural journalism to promote their development

"From-scratch" charter school—school that did not exist prior to its charter status

G

Gifted and talented student—student identified as having outstanding intellectual ability and/or creative talent

GOALS 2000: EDUCATE AMERICA Act—1994 federal statute that permits state educational agencies to use federal funds allotted for state and local education systematic improvement for promoting public charter schools

Governing board—site-based committee responsible for administering a charter school

H

High/Scope—curriculum focusing on the realization of key experiences through such active learning strategies as small groups and plan-do-review

Home school—school located in a home in which parents are the teachers

I

IASA—Improving America's Schools Act

IDEA—Individuals with Disabilities Education Act

IEP—individualized education program

Improving America's Schools Act of 1994—reauthorization of the federal Elementary and Secondary Education Act of 1965; see Titles I, II, IV, VI, VII, IX, and X, ESEA

Independent study—student design and implementation of a learning program with teacher facilitation

Individualized educational program—plan developed for a child with identified special needs which sets forth his/her current levels of performance, the goals to be achieved, the intervention to be provided, and the means of assessing attainment of the goals

Individuals with Disabilities Education Act—federal statute requiring that children with disabilities be provided a free appropriate education with individualized educational programs

Integrated thematic instruction—educational model that bases teaching strategies and curriculum development on brain research

International Baccalaureate program—International Baccalaureate Diploma Programme, a two year curriculum in which students complete courses in six subject areas, a Theory of Knowledge course, a Creativity, Action, Service requirement, and the writing of an extended essay; also a Middle Years Programme for students aged eleven to sixteen

J

Jacob K. Javits Gifted and Talented Students Education Act—federal program designed to meet the special educational needs of gifted and talented students: part of Title X, ESEA

Junior Great Books—K–12 curriculum coupling literature with interpretive discussion

K

Kids 1, Inc.—private firm which operates schools for special education and at-risk students with a program that emphasizes individualized instruction and behavior management

L

LEA—local education agency
LEP—limited-English proficient

M

Magnet school—alternative school
MAPSA—Michigan Association of Public School Academies
MEP—Migrant Education Program
Migrant Education Program—federal program addressing educational needs of migratory children; part of Title I, ESEA
Mission—school's vision: the goals to be attained and the philosophy and tenets driving the achievement of these goals
Modern Red Schoolhouse—educational design directed towards mastery of subject matter which incorporates individual education compacts, technology, and community involvement
Montessori—approach developed by Maria Montessori in which children learn at their own paces through their interactions with a prepared environment
MOU—memorandum of understanding
Multiple Intelligences—theory advanced by Howard Gardner that individuals have at least seven intelligences: linguistic, logical-mathematical, musical, spatial, bodily-kinesthetic, intrapersonal, and interpersonal

N

National Alliance for Restructuring Education—network of states, school districts, and schools subscribing to the Alliance's five design tasks and to the high standards which students must achieve to be awarded its Certificate of Initial Mastery

National Education Association—teachers' professional organization

National School Lunch Program—part of federal Child Nutrition program

NEA—National Education Association

New American Schools Development Corporation—nonprofit organization which promotes the development of seven educational improvement designs

Norm-referenced test—test in which a student's scores are compared with those of a sample group used to determine typical performance

NSLP—National School Lunch Program

O

Organizer—individual proposing a charter school

Outcome—learning objective

P

Paideia program—approach developed by Mortimer Adler in which learning occurs through the use of Socratic seminars, coached projects, and limited didactic instruction in a student-centered classroom

Performance assessment—assessment that occurs as a student functions in his/her school environment

Pilot school—alternative school

Portfolio—continuing collection of a student's work for the purpose of assessing progress

PPOR—per pupil operating revenue

Preoperational period—time between charter approval and school opening

Public Charter Schools program—authorization of federal grants for the planning and design of charter school educational programs, the establishment of state educational agency revolving loan funds to defray initial school operating costs, and the evaluation of charter school effects on student performance; part of Title X, ESEA

Public school academy—charter school (in Michigan)

R

Reggio Emilia—educational approach used in the schools of Reggio Emilia, Italy, in which children and teachers work together on long-term projects which emphasize the use of graphic representation

Risk management—measures instituted to assess and minimize potential risks and to provide appropriate insurance coverage

Roots and Wings—school design for infants through eleven year olds which emphasizes early learning programs, literacy, mathematics, and group social and scientific problem-solving

S

SABIS—international network of schools whose curriculum emphasizes math, English, world language, and science and which include a Student Life student organization

Safe and Drug-Free Schools and Communities Act—federal program providing grants for drug and violence prevention programs; Title IV, ESEA

SBM—site-based or school-based management

SEA—state educational agency

Section 504—section of the federal Rehabilitation Act of 1973 that bars agencies receiving federal funds from discriminating against any person because of his/her disability

Sending district—school district in which a student resides and would attend a public school

SES—socioeconomic status

Special education student—student with an identified disability who is entitled to receive specially designed instruction to meet his/her unique needs

Specialty school—alternative school

Sponsoring agency—public agency which grants, revokes, and renews charters and oversees charter school performance

Staffing—meeting at which a student's IEP is determined

Standardized test—norm-referenced test

Stewart B. McKinney Homeless Assistance Act—federal program designed to ensure that homeless children and youth have access to a free and appropriate public education

T
TBE—transitional bilingual education
Technical assistance provider—organization providing advice to charter school developers and charter schools
Title I, ESEA—authorization of federal funding designed to increase the achievement of poor and migratory children
Title II, ESEA—Dwight D. Eisenhower Professional Development Program
Title IV, ESEA—Safe and Drug-Free Schools and Communities Act
Title VI, ESEA—authorization of federal funding for such educational activities as literacy programs and programs for at-risk and gifted and talented children
Title VII, ESEA—federal program designed to increase the proficiency in English and the academic achievement of limited-English proficient students
Title IX, ESEA—federal program designed to promote the achievement of American Indian and Alaska Native children
Title X, ESEA—includes the Public Charter Schools program and the Jacob K. Javits Gifted and Talented Students Education Act

W
Waiver—exemption from a law or regulation
Waldorf Education—approach developed by Rudolf Steiner in which children develop through imitation in early childhood, imagination in middle childhood, and critical thought in adolescence and which includes an emphasis on the arts and practical skills
Warehousing—storage

Appendix B

··

References

Books, Reports, Articles, and Audiotapes

Abbott, Karen. "Relearning Education." *Denver Rocky Mountain News,* 27 October 1994.

Amole, Tustin. "Charter School Quest for Land, Building Fails." *Denver Rocky Mountain News,* 11 March 1997.

Anderson, Eric. "Charter School Moving." *Denver Post,* 10 June 1994.

Becker, Henry J., Kathryn Nakagawa, and Ronald G. Corwin. *Parent Involvement Contracts in California's Charter Schools: Strategy for Educational Improvement or Method of Exclusion?* April 1995. Los Alamitos, Calif.: Southwest Regional Laboratory, 1995.

Bierlein, Louann A., and Mary F. Fulton. "Emerging Issues in Charter School Financing." *Government Finance Review* 12 (August 1996): 25–27.

Bingham, Janet. "Denver's First Charter School To Close Down." *Denver Post,* 1 March 1997.

Buechler, Mark. *Charter Schools: Legislation and Results after Four Years,* Policy Report PR-B13, January 1996. Bloomington, Ind.: Indiana Education Policy Center, 1996.

BW Associates. *How Much Funding Should Charter Schools Receive?* Making Charters Work: Strategies for Charter School Developers, A Project of the California Business Roundtable, Brief #1, Winter 1994. Berkeley, Calif.: BW Associates, 1994a.

BW Associates. *Redesigning Education: Supporting the Charter Schools Movement,* Charter School Implementation Challenges, Discussion Paper #1, January 1994, WP-118. Berkeley, Calif.: BW Associates, 1994b.

BW Associates. *School Reform, Accountability, and Charter Schools,* Making Charters Work: Strategies for Charter School Developers, A Project of the California Business Roundtable, Brief #2, Spring 1994. Berkeley, Calif.: BW Associates, 1994c.

"CANEC's Characteristics of Strong Charter Petitions: A Handy Guide for Charter Developers and Renewers Alike." *CANECConnections,* (January 1997): 1–5.

Center for Education Reform. *Charter Schools around the Nation: Charter Schools Operating or Approved to Open, September 1997.* Washington, D.C.: Center for Education Reform, 1997a.

Center for Education Reform. *Special Profile: Status of Charter Schools and Laws, April, 1997.* Washington, D.C.: Center for Education Reform, 1997b.

Chan, Yvonne. *Keynote Address, 1997 California Conference on Charter Schools.* (April 11, 1997): audiotape.

Chubb, John E., and Terry M. Moe. *Politics, Markets, and America's Schools.* Washington, D.C.: Brookings Institution, 1990.

Clayton Foundation, and Center for Human Investment Policy at The University of Colorado at Denver. *The Colorado Charter Schools Evaluation, Prepared for Colorado Department of Education, March 1997.* 1997.

Clinton, William J. *Remarks by the President in State of the Union Address, United States Capitol, February 4, 1997.* 1997.

Colorado Department of Education. *Trends in Colorado Public School Membership from 1980 to 1996.* Denver: Colorado Department of Education, 1996.

"Colorado Charter School Study Commission." *Charter School Bulletin* [Colorado Department of Education] 2 (January 1996): 1–4.

Commonwealth of Massachusetts, Department of Education. *Application for a Public School Charter, 1997-1998.* Boston: Massachusetts Department of Education, 1997a.

Commonwealth of Massachusetts, Department of Education. *The Massachusetts Charter School Initiative 1996 Report.* Boston: Massachusetts Department of Education, 1997b.

Commonwealth of Massachusetts, Department of Education. *Massachusetts Charter School Law and Draft Regulations.* Boston: Massachusetts Department of Education, 1997c.

Commonwealth of Massachusetts, Executive Office of Education. *Charter School Application, 1996.* Boston: Executive Office of Education, 1996.

Dale, Angela H., ed. *National Charter School Directory, Fall 1996,* 3rd Ed. Washington, D.C.: Center for Education Reform, 1996.

Democratic Leadership Council. *Blueprint for Change: Charter Schools: A Handbook for Action.* Washington, D.C.: Democratic Leadership Council, n.d.

Dianda, Marcella R., and Ronald G. Corwin. *Vision and Reality: A First-Year Look at California's Charter Schools, May 1994.* Los Alamitos, Calif.: Southwest Regional Laboratory, 1994.

Education Commission of the States. *A Guide to New American Schools.* Denver: Education Commission of the States, 1996.

"Educational Process Defined." *Charter School Bulletin* [Colorado Department of Education] 1 (November/December 1994): 1–2.

"Excel Academy to Receive Grant." *Lakewood (Colorado) Jefferson Sentinel,* 29 February 1996.

Finn, Chester E., Jr., Bruno V. Manno, and Louann Bierlein. *Charter Schools in Action: What Have We Learned?* Indianapolis: Hudson Institute, Educational Excellence Network, 1996.

Fitzgerald, Joy. *Charter Schools in Colorado, March, 1995.* Denver: Colorado Children's Campaign, 1995.

Gifford, Mary. *Arizona's Charter Schools: A Survey of Parents, April 1996,* Arizona Issue Analysis #140. Phoenix: Goldwater Institute, 1996.

Gifford, Mary, and Timothy Keller. *Arizona's Charter Schools: A Survey of Teachers, August 1996,* Arizona Issue Analysis #141. Phoenix: Goldwater Institute, 1996.

Grantier, Virginia. "Modular Classroom Puts Kids in Business World." *Denver Post,* 26 June 1995.

Hart, Gary. *Charter Schools: Where Have We Been? Where Are We Going? A State Perspective!,* California Network of Educational Charters (CANEC) 1995 Conference Closing Address. 1995.

Horowitz, Steven. "Be Your Own Reporter." *Thrust for Educational Leadership* (January 1996): 18–23.

Jefferson County School District R-1. *District Accountability. Charter School Guidelines and Application Procedures, August 1, 1996.* 1996.

Lange, Cheryl, Camilla Lehr, Patricia Seppanen, and Mary Sinclair. *Minnesota Charter Schools Evaluation: Interim Report, December 1996.* Minneapolis: CAREI, 1996.

Little Hoover Commission. *The Charter Movement: Education Reform School by School, March 1996.* Sacramento, Calif.: Little Hoover Commission, 1996.

McKinney, Joseph R. "Charter Schools: A New Barrier for Children with Disabilities." *Educational Leadership* 54 (October 1996): 22–25.

McQuade, Finlay, and David W. Champagne. *How to Make a Better School.* Boston: Allyn and Bacon, 1995.

Marketing and Fundraising, 1997 California Conference on Charter Schools, Session 5D. (April 12, 1997): audiotape.

Medler, Alex, and Joe Nathan. *Charter Schools...What Are They Up To?: A 1995 Survey, August 1995.* Denver: Education Commission of the States and Minneapolis: Center for School Change, Humphrey Institute of Public Affairs, University of Minnesota, 1995.

Merriam-Webster's Collegiate Dictionary. 10th Ed. Springfield, Mass.: Merriam-Webster, Incorporated, 1996.

Michigan Association of Public School Academies (MAPSA). *Advancing Michigan's Charter Schools.* Lansing, Mich.: Michigan Association of Public School Academies, n.d.

Millot, Marc Dean, and Robin J. Lake, reporters. *So You Want to Start a Charter School? Strategic Advice for Applicants: Recommendations from an Expert Workshop, October 1996.* Seattle: University of Washington, Graduate School of Public Affairs, Institute for Public Policy and Management, and RAND Institute for Education and Training. 1996.

Mulholland, Lori A., and Louann A. Bierlein. *Understanding Charter Schools,* Fastback 383. Bloomington, Ind.: Phi Delta Kappa Educational Foundation, 1995.

Nathan, Joe. *Charter Schools: Creating Hope and Opportunity for American Education.* San Francisco: Jossey-Bass Publishers, 1996.

National Education Association, Center for Advancement of Public Education. "Charter Schools Action Section." In *The People's Cause: Mobilizing for Public Education.* Washington, D.C.: National Education Association, 1995.

"National News Notes." *CANECConnections* (May-June 1997): 6.

Page, Linda, with Mark Levine. "The Pitfalls and Triumphs of Launching a Charter School." *Educational Leadership* 54 (October 1996): 26-29.

Patterson, David. "Charter School Update—January 1997." *CANECConnections* (January 1997): 5–7.

Pearson, Hugh. "An Urban Push for Self-Reliance." *Wall Street Journal,* 7 February 1996.

Pioneer Institute for Public Policy Research, Charter School Resource Center. *The Massachusetts Charter School Handbook, March 1996,* 2nd Ed. Boston: Pioneer Institute for Public Policy Research, 1996.

Ponessa, Jeanne. "Star Potential: At Constellation Community Middle School—a Principal-Free Charter School in California—Teachers and Students Think They Have What It Takes to Give Education Top Billing." *Education Week* 16 (13 November 1996): 28–33.

Premack, Eric. *Labor Relations and California Charter Schools,* Making Charters Work: Strategies for Charter School Developers, The Charter Schools Project, Brief #3, Summer 1995. Berkeley, Calif.: Institute for Policy Analysis and Research, 1995.

Premack, Eric. *California Charter School Revenues: A Guide for Charter Schools and Sponsor Districts,* 1996–97 Ed. 1997a.

Premack, Eric. *Charter School Development Guide, 1997 California Edition.* 1997b.

A Profile of California's Charter Schools, 1994–95: A Project of the San Diego Chamber of Commerce Business Roundtable for Education and Charter Schools Consortium, March 1996. San Diego: Greater San Diego Chamber of Commerce, 1996.

"P.S. 1 Rejects Denver Offer." *Denver Rocky Mountain News,* 9 April 1995.

RPP International, and University of Minnesota. *A Study of Charter Schools, First-Year Report, 1997.* Washington, D.C.: U. S. Department of Education, Office of Educational Research and Improvement, 1997.

Scanlon, Bill. "Attention Turns to Edison School Debut." *Denver Rocky Mountain News,* 28 August 1996. (1996a)

Scanlon, Bill. "Students Are Learning Their Way." *Denver Rocky Mountain News,* 2 October 1996. (1996 b)

Schnaiberg, Lynn. "Charter School Laws Are All over the Map on Disabled Students." *Education Week* 16 (19 February 1997): 25.

Schneider, Joe, and Marcella Dianda. "Coping with Charters; Savvy Leaders Can Work Productively with Charter School Advocates." *School Administrator* 52 (August 1995): 20–23.

Stevens, Mark. "Charter Bid OK'd—with Ifs." *Denver Post,* 21 April 1995.

Sweeney, Mary Ellen, and Jesus Garcia. "Implementing a Charter School: One Colorado Group's Experience: Several Lessons Learned." *Changing Schools* 23 (February 1995): 1–5.

Thomas, Doug. "The Choice to Charter: Why One School Board Decided to Sponsor a Charter School." *American School Board Journal* 183 (July 1996): 20–22.

U.S. Congress, House of Representatives, Committee on Education and the Workforce, Subcommittee on Early Childhood, Youth and Families. *Hearing on Charter Schools: Hearing before the Subcommittee on Early Childhood, Youth and Families.* 105th Cong., 1st sess., 9 April 1997. Washington, D.C.: U.S. Government Printing Office, 1997.

U.S. Department of Education. *Guide to the U.S. Department of Education Programs*. Washington, D.C.: U. S. Department of Education, 1997.

U.S. Department of Education, WestEd, and California State University Institute for Education Reform. *US Charter Schools Web Site*. (http://www.uscharterschools.org)

University of Minnesota, Humphrey Institute of Public Affairs, Center for School Change. *Parent/Community Involvement Opportunities: Fifty Ideas*. Minneapolis: Center for School Change, n.d.

Urahn, Sue, and Dan Stewart. *Minnesota Charter Schools: A Research Report, December 1994*. St. Paul, MN: Minnesota House of Representatives, Research Department, 1994.

"Useful Tidbits." *Charter School Bulletin* [Colorado Department of Education] 1 (October 1994): 3.

Vanourek, Gregg, Bruno V. Manno, Chester E. Finn, Jr., and Louann A. Bierlein. *Charter Schools as Seen by Those Who Know Them Best: Students, Teachers, and Parents,* Charter Schools in Action, Final Report, Part I, June 1997. Washington, D.C.: Hudson Institute, 1997a.

Vanourek, Gregg, Bruno V. Manno, Chester E. Finn, Jr., and Louann A. Bierlein. *The Educational Impact of Charter Schools,* Charter Schools in Action, Final Report, Part V, July 1997. Washington, D.C.: Hudson Institute, 1997b.

Vergari, Sandra, and Michael Mintrom. *Charter Schools Laws across the United States: A Policy Report, September 1996*. 1996 Ed. East Lansing, Mich: Michigan State University, Institute for Public Policy and Social Research, 1996.

Wallis, Claudia. "A Class of Their Own: Bucking Bureaucracy, Brashly Independent Public Schools Have Much to Teach about Saving Education." *Time,* 31 October 1994, 52–61.

Webster's Encyclopedic Unabridged Dictionary of the English Language. New York: Portland House, 1989.

Weiss, Abby R. *Going It Alone: A Study of Massachusetts Charter Schools, March 1997*. Boston: Northeastern University, Institute for Responsive Education, 1997.

Wilson, Wendy. "School's Turmoil Laid to Control Fight." *Riverside (California) Press-Enterprise,* 10 June 1997.

Windler, William, ed. *Colorado Charter School Information Packet and Handbook, The Colorado Charter Schools Act of 1993, September 1997,* 5th Ed. Denver: Colorado Department of Education, 1997.

Wisconsin Association of School Boards. *Charter Schools in Wisconsin, September 1996.* Madison, Wisc: Wisconsin Association of School Boards, 1996.

Interviews

Ballantine, Mary Lyn, The EXCEL School, Durango, Colorado, December 5, 1996.

Booth, Cordia, proposed Thurgood Marshall Charter Middle School, Denver, Colorado, December 9, 1996.

Brown, Rexford, P.S. 1, Denver, Colorado, January 2, 1997.

Brunnig, Sarah, home school parent, January 24, 1997.

Elliot, Sandra. Roosevelt-Edison Charter School, Colorado Springs, Colorado, December 19, 1996.

Hamilton-Pennell, Robert, proposed Discovery Charter School, Aurora, Colorado, January 15, 1997.

Jaramillo, Ginny, Lake George-Guffey Charter School, Lake George, Colorado, December 2, 1996.

Levine, Mark, Swallows Charter Academy, Pueblo West, Colorado, December 6, 1996.

Mani, Meera, Clayton Foundation, Denver, Colorado, December 18, 1996

Mikulas, Judy, The Connect School, Pueblo, Colorado, December 4, 1996.

Pantleo, Sam, Pueblo School for the Arts and Sciences, Pueblo, Colorado, January 16, 1997.

Rodriguez, Ray, Community Prep School, Colorado Springs, Colorado, January 29, 1997.

Van Manen, Dave, home school parent, January 10, 1997.

Appendix C

....

Resources

Accountability

BW Associates. *School Reform, Accountability, and Charter Schools,*
Making Charters Work: Strategies for Charter School Developers,
A Project of the California Business Roundtable, Brief #2, Spring
1994. Berkeley, Calif.: BW Associates, 1994.
Information on determining measurable school outcomes,
the means to attain them, and the methods of assessing them.
Available from:
Institute for Policy Analysis and Research
2200 Powell Street, Suite 250-A
Emeryville, CA 94608
Tel: 510-450-2555; Fax: 510-450-0113

Commonwealth of Massachusetts, Executive Office of Education.
Public School Reporting Guide for Charter Schools, 1995–1996.
Boston: Executive Office of Education. n.d.
A reporting guide for Massachusetts charter schools that
could be used by other charter schools as they develop systems
to meet their states' reporting requirements.
Available from:
Massachusetts Executive Office of Education
One Ashburton Place, Room 1401
Boston, MA 02108
Tel: 617-727-0075; Fax: 617-727-0049

Curricula/Instructional Approaches

American Montessori Society
281 Park Avenue South, Sixth Floor
New York, NY 10010-6102
Tel: 212-358-1250; Fax: 212-358-1256

Association Montessori Internationale
410 Alexander Street
Rochester, NY, 14607
Tel: 716-461-5920

Association of Waldorf Schools of North America
3911 Bannister Road
Fair Oaks, CA, 95628
Tel: 916-961-0927; Fax: 916-961-0715

CATO
P.O. Box 720069
Pinon Hills, CA 92372-0069
Tel: 619-868-4108; Fax: 619-868-2051

Character Education Partnership
918 16th Street, NW, Suite 501
Washington, DC 20006
Tel: 202-296-7743; Fax: 202-296-7779

Coalition of Essential Schools
Box 1969, Brown University
Providence, RI 02912
Tel: 401-863-3384; Fax: 401-863-2045

Core Knowledge Foundation
2012-B Morton Drive
Charlottesville, VA 22903
Tel: 800-238-3233; Fax: 804-977-0021

Education Commission of the States. *A Guide to New American Schools.*
Denver: Education Commission of the States, 1996.
A description of the seven educational designs of New American Schools: ATLAS Communities, The Audrey Cohen College System of Education, Co-NECT Schools, Expeditionary Learning Outward Bound, Modern Red Schoolhouse, National Alliance for Restructuring Education, and Roots and Wings. Available from:
ECS Distribution Center
707 17th Street, Suite 2700
Denver, CO 80202-3427
Tel: 303-299-3692

Efficacy Institute
128 Spring Street
Lexington, MA 02173
Tel: 617-862-4390; Fax: 617-862-2580

The Galef Institute (Different Ways of Knowing: DWoK)
11050 Santa Monica Boulevard, Third Floor
Los Angeles, CA 90025
Tel: 310-479-8883; Fax: 310-473-9720

The Great Books Foundation (Junior Great Books)
35 East Wacker Drive, Suite 2300
Chicago, IL 60601-2298
Tel: 800-222-5870; Fax: 312-407-0334

High/Scope Educational Research Foundation
600 North River Street
Ypsilanti, MI 48198-2898
Tel: 313-485-2000; Fax: 313-485-0704

International Baccalaureate North America
200 Madison Avenue, Suite 2007
New York, NY 10016
Tel: 212-696-4464; Fax: 212-889-9242

National Center for the Accelerated Schools Project
Center for Educational Research at Stanford,
School of Education, Stanford University
Stanford, CA 94305-3084
Tel: 415-725-1676; Fax: 415-723-7578

National Paideia Center
The University of North Carolina at Chapel Hill
Campus Box 8045
Chapel Hill, NC 27599
Tel: 919-962-7379; Fax: 919-962-738

Project Zero Development Group (Multiple Intelligences)
Harvard Graduate School of Education
323 Longfellow Hall
Cambridge, MA 02138
Tel: 617-495-4342; Fax: 617-495-9709

Puckett, John L. *Foxfire Reconsidered: A Twenty-Year Experiment in Progressive Education.* Urbana, IL: University of Illinois Press, 1989.

Reggio Children/USA
    2460 16th Street, NW
    Washington, DC 20009-3575
    Tel: 202-265-9090; Fax: 202-265-9161

Susan Kovalik and Associates (Integrated Thematic Instruction)
    17051 SE 272nd St., Suite 17
    Kent, WA 98042
    Tel: 206-631-4400; Fax: 206-631-7500

Wigginton, Eliot. *Sometimes a Shining Moment: The Foxfire Experience.*
    Garden City, NY: Anchor Press/Doubleday, 1985.

Directories

Clayton Foundation, and Center for Human Investment Policy at The
    University of Colorado at Denver. *The Colorado Charter Schools
    Evaluation, Prepared for Colorado Department of Education, March 1997.*
        An evaluation of fourteen Colorado charter schools that
    includes information on their individual missions, educational
    programs, student profiles, governance, performance goals, and
    student achievement results.
    Available from:
    Colorado Department of Education, State Office Building
    201 East Colfax Avenue
    Denver, CO 80203

Commonwealth of Massachusetts, Department of Education. *The
    Massachusetts Charter School Initiative 1996 Report.* Boston:
    Massachusetts Department of Education, 1997.
        Profiles of individual Massachusetts charter schools that
    include photographs of their buildings and information on their
    missions, origins, programs, and statistical profiles.
    Available from:
    Massachusetts Department of Education, Boston Office
    One Ashburton Place, Room 1403
    Boston, MA 02108
    Tel: 617-727-0075

Dale, Angela H., ed. *National Charter School Directory, Fall 1996,* 3rd Ed.
    Washington, D.C.: Center for Education Reform, 1996.
        A listing by state of 480 current and 32 approved, but not yet
    opened charter schools, showing their addresses, telephone

numbers, contact persons, opening dates, grade spans, enrollments, and distinguishing characteristics. Also listed are charter school organizations and resources.
Available from:
Center for Education Reform
1001 Connecticut Avenue, NW, Suite 204
Washington, DC 20036
Tel: 800-521-2118; Fax: 202-822-5077

Kolderie, Ted. *A Guide to Charter Activity (August 1996)*. St. Paul, Minn.: Center for Policy Studies, 1996.
A state-by-state guide with the names and phone numbers of legislators, government staff, and others involved with charter schools as well as information on school directories, electronic discussions, recent research, and organizations and individuals active in the charter school movement.
Available from:
Center for Policy Studies
59 West Fourth Street
St. Paul MN 55102
Tel: 612-224-9703

Lange, Cheryl et al. *Minnesota Charter Schools Evaluation: Interim Report, December 1996*. Minneapolis: CAREI, 1996.
This report includes descriptive pages on sixteen Minnesota charter schools.
Available from:
Center for Applied Research and Educational Improvement
College of Education and Human Development
University of Minnesota, 265-2 Peik Hall
159 Pillsbury Drive, S.E.
Minneapolis, MN 55455-0208
Tel: 612-625-6364; Fax: 612-625-3086

Morasky, Angela. *Wisconsin Charter Schools*. Madison, WI: Wisconsin Department of Public Instruction, 1997.
A description of Wisconsin's existing charter school programs.
Available from:
Angela Morasky
1781 Dickson Drive
Sun Prairie, WI 53590
Tel: 608-825-7466

Pioneer Institute for Public Policy Research, Charter School Resource
Center. *Massachusetts Charter School Profiles, 1996–97 School Year,
Interim Report, March 1997.* Boston: Pioneer Institute for Public
Policy Research, 1997.

Two-page descriptions of individual Massachusetts charter
schools that include information on distinctive features, teaching
method, demand, performance, and budget. (Web site:
http://www.pioneerinstitute.org)

*A Profile of California's Charter Schools, 1994-95: A Project of the San
Diego Chamber of Commerce Business Roundtable for Education and
Charter Schools Consortium, March 1996.* San Diego: Greater San
Diego Chamber of Commerce, 1996.

Two-page descriptions of 43 California charter schools that
for each school presents a general overview, student demograph-
ics and assessment methods, major successes and distinguishing
features, and major obstacles and concerns.
Available from:
Greater San Diego Chamber of Commerce
Business Roundtable for Education
Emerald Shapery Center
402 West Broadway, Suite 1000
San Diego, CA 92101-3585
Tel. 619-544-1391; Fax. 619-234-0571

Finances

BW Associates. *How Much Funding Should Charter Schools Receive?*
Making Charters Work: Strategies for Charter School Developers,
A Project of the California Business Roundtable, Brief #1, Winter
1994. Berkeley, Calif.: BW Associates, 1994.

A look at the funding issues which California charter schools
face that includes suggestions generally applicable to those estab-
lishing charter schools.
Available from:
Institute for Policy Analysis and Research
2200 Powell Street, Suite 250-A
Emeryville, CA 94608
Tel: 510-450-2555; Fax: 510-450-0113

Premack, Eric. *California Charter School Revenues: A Guide for Charter
Schools and Sponsor Districts, 1996-97 Ed, 1997.*
A detailed explanation and discussion of charter school fiscal

management that should also be helpful to charter school developers in other states.
Available from:
Charter Schools Project
California State University Institute for Education Reform
6000 J Street
Sacramento, CA 95819-6018
Tel: 916-278-4600

U.S. Department of Education. *Guide to the U.S. Department of Education Programs.* Washington, D.C.: U. S. Department of Education, 1997.
Guide to U.S. Department of Education programs which includes information on the program, who may apply, the type of assistance, the educational levels, and contact information.
Available from:
U. S. Department of Education
Office of Public Affairs, Editorial Services and Policy Branch
600 Independence Avenue, SW
Washington, DC 20202
Tel: 202-401-1576 or 202-401-1311
Web site: http://www.ed.gov/

For-Profit School Management Companies

Beacon Education Management
28 White Bridge Road, Suite 311
Nashville, TN 37205
Tel: 800-789-1258; Fax: 615-352-2138

The Edison Project
521 Fifth Avenue, 16th Floor
New York, NY 10175
Tel: 212-309-1658, ext. 1113

Kids 1, Inc.
10 Auer Court, Suite G
East Brunswick, NJ 08816
Tel: 908-390-0303; Fax: 908-390-5577

SABIS Educational Systems, Inc.
6385 Beach Road
Eden Prairie, MN 55344
Tel: 612-829-9352; Fax: 612-941-4015

General

Arizona Department of Education. *Arizona Charter Schools: Charter Schools Handbook, April 1997.* Phoenix: Arizona Department of Education, 1997.
   A large compilation of legislation, regulations, and information specifically applicable to Arizona charter schools that can give charter school developers in states which do not yet have such a handbook a view of the areas they may need to address.
Available from:
Charter Schools Administration Office
Arizona Department of Education
1535 West Jefferson Street
Phoenix, AZ 85007
Tel: 602-542-4361

BW Associates. *Redesigning Education: Supporting the Charter Schools Movement,* Charter School Implementation Challenges, Discussion Paper #1, January 1994, WP-118. Berkeley, Calif.: BW Associates, 1994.
   A presentation of issues facing charter school developers in California that should be of general interest.
Available from:
Institute for Policy Analysis and Research
2200 Powell Street, Suite 250-A
Emeryville, CA 94608
Tel: 510-450-2555; Fax: 510-450-0113

Commonwealth of Massachusetts, Executive Office of Education. *Charter School Application, 1996.* Boston: Executive Office of Education, 1996.
   A guide for Massachusetts charter school applicants that notes under each subheading of the application what specifics are being sought and contains Massachusetts' legislation, regulations, and guidelines as well as assistance sources.
Available from:
Massachusetts Executive Office of Education
One Ashburton Place, Room 1401
Boston, MA 02108
Tel: 617-727-0075; Fax: 617-727-0049

DeRaad, Carolyn G., ed. *Guidebook to Colorado Charter Schools: Key Issues for Start-up and Implementation of Charter Schools—Sample Documents Included, Prepared by the Colorado Children's Campaign for the Colorado Department of Education, August, 1997.* Denver: Colorado Department of Education, 1997.

A large loose-leaf guidebook that provides information and sample documents on charter school applications and implementation that should prove invaluable for charter schools in Colorado and in other states.
Available from:
Colorado Department of Education, State Office Building
201 East Colfax Avenue
Denver, CO 80203
Tel: 303-866-6631

Ducote, Jacklyn. *Louisiana Charter School Handbook.* Baton Rouge: Public Affairs Research Council of Louisiana, 1997.

This guidebook includes information on frequently asked questions, federal grants, and information sources.
Available from:
Public Affairs Research Council of Louisiana
P.O. Box 14776
Baton Rouge, LA 70898-4776
Tel: 504-926-8414; Fax: 504-926-8417

Finn, Chester E., Jr., Bruno V. Manno, and Louann Bierlein. *Charter Schools in Action: What Have We Learned?* Indianapolis: Hudson Institute, Educational Excellence Network, 1996.

An in-depth study of thirty-five charter schools in seven states that analyzes the start-up problems they encountered and explores solutions.
Available from:
Hudson Institute, Herman Kahn Center
P.O. Box 26-919
Indianapolis, IN 46226
Tel: 800-483-7660

Fitzgerald, Joy. *Charter Schools in Colorado, March, 1995.* Denver: Colorado Children's Campaign, 1995.

A report that includes a checklist of seventeen suggestions garnered from responses of those involved in the charter school application process.
Available from:
Colorado Children's Campaign
1600 Sherman Street B-300
Denver, CO 80203
Tel: 303-839-1580

Jefferson County School District R-1, District Accountability. *Charter School Guidelines and Application Procedures, August 1, 1996*. 1996.
A working document for charter schools in Colorado's R-1 school district that includes information on the application, renewal and appeal processes; an application checklist; material on required school improvement plans; and a budget worksheet. Available from:
Jefferson County Public Schools
Area Administrator for Districtwide Schools
P.O. Box 4001
Golden, CO 80401-0001
Tel: 303-982-6939

Lange, Cheryl et al. *Minnesota Charter Schools Evaluation: Interim Report, December 1996*. Minneapolis: CAREI, 1996.
An evaluation based on the experiences of sixteen Minnesota charter schools that offers helpful insights to charter school operators. Available from:
Center for Applied Research and Educational Improvement
College of Education and Human Development
University of Minnesota, 265-2 Peik Hall
159 Pillsbury Drive, S.E.
Minneapolis, MN 55455-0208
Tel: 612-625-6364; Fax: 612-625-3086

Little Hoover Commission. *The Charter Movement: Education Reform School by School, March 1996*. Sacramento, Calif.: Little Hoover Commission, 1996.
A study of California's charter schools that includes its findings on charter autonomy, funding, roadblocks, and success. Available from:
Little Hoover Commission
660 J Street, Suite 260
Sacramento, CA 95814
Tel: 916-445-2125; Fax 916-322-7709

Millot, Marc Dean, and Robin J. Lake, reporters. *So You Want to Start a Charter School? Strategic Advice for Applicants: Recommendations from an Expert Workshop, October 1996*. Seattle: University of Washington, Graduate School of Public Affairs, Institute for Public Policy and Management, and RAND Institute for Education and Training. 1996.

A synthesis of the constructive recommendations presented by twelve experts during a conference in Seattle on the business aspects of starting a charter school.
Available from:
Program on Reinventing Public Education
Institute for Public Policy and Management
Box 353060, University of Washington
Seattle, WA 98195
Tel: 206-685-2214; Fax: 206-616-5769

Millot, Marc Dean, with Robin Lake. *Supplying a System of Charter Schools: Observations on Early Implementation of the Massachusetts Statute, June 1997.* Seattle: UW/RAND Program on Reinventing Public Education, 1997.

An examination of the development of charter schools in Massachusetts that looks at the motivations and capabilities of different types of charter applicants and at the barriers which posed the most significant problems for these groups.
Available from:
Institute for Public Policy and Management
Box 353060, University of Washington
Seattle, WA 98195
Tel: 206-685-2214; Fax: 206-616-5769

Minnesota New Country School, Planning Committee and Board of Education. *Design Plan Overview.* LeSueur, MN; Minnesota New Country School, 1996.

A school design document developed by a charter school which has been in operation since 1994.
Available from:
Minnesota New Country School
115 North Main Street
LeSueur, MN 56058
Tel: 507-665-4033

Mulholland, Lori A., and Louann A. Bierlein. *Understanding Charter Schools,* Fastback 383. Bloomington, Ind.: Phi Delta Kappa Educational Foundation, 1995.

An introduction to charter schools that includes information on the approval process, five sample charter school programs, and issues faced by charter school developers.
Available from:

Phi Delta Kappa Educational Foundation
408 N. Union, P.O. Box 789
Bloomington, IN 47402-0789
Tel: 812-339-1156

Nathan, Joe. *Charter Schools: Creating Hope and Opportunity for American Education.* San Francisco: Jossey-Bass Publishers, 1996.
    An excellent overall book on charter schools, which discusses the concept, the history and future of the movement, the challenges faced by charter schools, specific charter schools, and state legislation. Three chapters offer valuable advice for those starting charter schools.
Available through local bookstores.

Novato Unified School District. *Agreement between The Novato Unified School District and The Novato Charter School.* n.d.
    An example of an agreement between a charter school and its sponsoring agency.
Available from:
Novato Charter School
601 Bolling Drive
Novato, CA 94945
Tel: 415-883-4254

Pioneer Institute for Public Policy Research, Charter School Resource Center. *The Massachusetts Charter School Handbook, March 1996,* 2nd Ed. Boston: Pioneer Institute for Public Policy Research, 1996.
    A handbook that contains a wealth of information that would be a useful resource for those involved with charter schools in Massachusetts and elsewhere. (Web site: http://www.pioneerinstitute.org)

Premack, Eric. *Charter School Development Guide, 1997 California Edition.* 1997.
    A manual on developing charter schools from inception to start-up whose detailed information should be useful to charter school developers regardless of their location.
Available from:
Charter Schools Project
California State University Institute for Education Reform
6000 J Street
Sacramento, CA 95819-6018
Tel: 916-278-4600

RPP International, and University of Minnesota. *A Study of Charter Schools, First-Year Report, 1997.* Washington, DC: U.S. Department of Education, Office of Educational Research and Improvement, 1997.

First year progress report of the U.S. Department of Education's National Study of Charter Schools that provides information on the characteristics of existing charter schools and on the factors that have hindered their development and implementation.
Available from:
Information Resource Center, U.S. Department of Education
600 Independence Avenue, SW
Washington, DC 20202
Tel: 202-401-2000

U.S. Congress, House of Representatives, Committee on Education and the Workforce, Subcommittee on Early Childhood, Youth and Families. *Hearing on Charter Schools: Hearing before the Subcommittee on Early Childhood, Youth and Families. 105th Cong., 1st sess., 9 April 1997.* Washington, DC: U.S. Government Printing Office, 1997.

Congressional hearing on the charter school movement and the federal Public Charter Schools program.
Available from:
U.S. Government Printing Office, Superintendent of Documents
P.O. Box 371954
Pittsburgh, PA 15250-7954
Tel: 202-512-1808; Fax: 202-512-2225—refer to GPO Stock Number: 552-070-21146-2

U.S. Department of Education, WestEd, and California State University Institute for Education Reform. *US Charter School Web Site.*

This national web site has four major components: starting and running your school, school information exchange, resource directory and links, and search other charter school sites. (http://www.uscharterschools.org)

Vanourek, Gregg, Bruno V. Manno, Chester E. Finn, Jr., and Louann A. Bierlein. *Charter Schools as Seen by Those Who Know Them Best: Students, Teachers, and Parents, Charter Schools in Action, Final Report, Part I,* June 1997. Washington, D.C.: Hudson Institute, 1997.

The results of a survey of charter school parents, students, and teachers that describes the reasons for their selection of char-

ter schools, the extent of their satisfaction, and the demographics of the charter school population.
Available from:
Hudson Institute
1015 18th Street, NW, Suite 300
Washington, DC 20036
Tel: 800-483-7660

Vanourek, Gregg, Bruno V. Manno, Chester E. Finn, Jr., and Louann A. Bierlein. *The Educational Impact of Charter Schools,* Charter Schools in Action, Final Report, Part V, July 1997. Washington, D.C.: Hudson Institute, 1997.
    A report on the educational impact of charter schools on students (including those who are at-risk or have IEP's), on parents, on teachers, and on communities.
Available from:
Hudson Institute
1015 18th Street, NW, Suite 300
Washington, DC 20036
Tel: 800-483-7660

Weiss, Abby R. *Going It Alone: A Study of Massachusetts Charter Schools, March 1997.* Boston: Northeastern University, Institute for Responsive Education, 1997.
    A perceptive look at the experiences of five Massachusetts charter schools.
Available from:
Institute for Responsive Education
Northeastern University
50 Nightingale Hall
Boston, MA 02115
Tel: 617-373-2595; Fax: 617-373-8924
Website:http: // www2.dac.neu.edu / Units / ArtsSci / IRE

Windler, William, ed. *Colorado Charter School Information Packet and Handbook, The Colorado Charter Schools Act of 1993, September 1996,* 4th Ed. Denver: Colorado Department of Education, 1997.
    An information packet whose resource listing and detailed information on preparing applications have general applicability.
Available from:
Colorado Department of Education, State Office Building
201 East Colfax Avenue
Denver, CO 80203
Tel: 303-866-6631

Labor Relations/Staff

Gifford, Mary and Timothy Keller. *Arizona's Charter Schools: A Survey of Teachers, August 1996,* Arizona Issue Analysis #141. Phoenix: Goldwater Institute, 1996.

Results from a survey of 120 Arizona charter school teachers that should be helpful to charter school developers both by identifying a number of organizational areas which should be addressed and by providing insights on charter school teachers' experiences.
Available from:
Goldwater Institute
Bank One Center-Concourse
201 N. Central Avenue
Phoenix, AZ 85004
Tel: 602-256-7018; Fax: 602-256-7045

Premack, Eric. *Labor Relations and California Charter Schools,* Making Charters Work: Strategies for Charter School Developers, The Charter Schools Project, Brief #3, Summer 1995. Berkeley, Calif.: Institute for Policy Analysis and Research, 1995.

A brief, that in addition to discussing California's teacher petition requirement, describes charter school collective bargaining issues and provides suggestions for charter school applicants.
Available from:
Institute for Policy Analysis and Research
2200 Powell Street, Suite 250-A
Emeryville, CA 94608
Tel: 510-450-2555; Fax: 510-450-0113

Legislation

Buechler, Mark. *Charter Schools: Legislation and Results after Four Years,* Policy Report PR-B13, January 1996. Bloomington, Ind.: Indiana Education Policy Center, 1996.

A comparison of charter school laws that discusses the expansive/restrictive characteristics of each state's legislation.
Available from:
Indiana Education Policy Center, School of Education Office
Smith Center for Research in Education:
Suite 170, Indiana University
Bloomington, IN 47408-2698
Tel: 812-855-1240; Fax: 812-855-0420

Center for Education Reform. *Special Profile: Status of Charter Schools and Laws, April, 1997.* Washington, D.C.: Center for Education Reform, 1997.

A ranking of the statutes of twenty-five states and the District of Columbia on each of ten criteria as well as on their overall strength.
Available from:
The Center for Education Reform
1001 Connecticut Avenue, NW, Suite 204
Washington, DC 20036
Tel.: 800-521-2118; Fax: 202-822-5077

Vergari, Sandra, and Michael Mintrom. *Charter Schools Laws across the United States: A Policy Report, September 1996.* 1996 Ed. East Lansing, Mich.: Michigan State University, Institute for Public Policy and Social Research, 1996.

A summary of the charter school laws of twenty-five states and the District of Columbia that for each state covers nine components: organization, sponsorship, legal status, regulations, accountability, admissions, funding, teachers, and number.
Available from:
Michigan State University Institute for Public Policy and Social Research
321 Berkey Hall
East Lansing, MI 48824-1111
Tel: 517-355-6672

Weiss, Abby R., and Nancy Sconyers. *A National Survey and Analysis of Charter School Legislation, A Report to the Citizens of the State of Connecticut, February 1, 1996.* Boston: Institute for Responsive Education, 1996.

A report on the charter school laws of eleven states that analyzes the areas of funding, contract and approval process, teachers, admissions, and outcomes.
Available from:
Institute for Responsive Education
Northeastern University
50 Nightingale Hall
Boston, MA 02115
Tel: 617-373-2595; Fax: 617-373-8924

Networks

Arizona Charter Schools Association
    ACSA/Intelli School
    10410 N. 31st Avenue, Suite 401
    Phoenix, AZ 85051
    Tel: 602-897-9365

California Network of Educational Charters (CANEC)
    751 Laurel St., Box 414
    San Carlos, CA 94070-3122
    Tel: 415-598-8192; Fax: 415-591-1043

Charter Friends National Network
    1355 Pierce Butler Route, #100
    St. Paul, MN 55104
    Tel: 612-644-5270; Fax: 612-645-0240

Citizen Alliance for Choice in Education
    Box 767
    Acton, MA 01720
    Tel: 508-635-1800; Fax: 508-635-1804

Colorado League of Charter Schools
    7700 W. Woodard Drive
    Lakewood, CO 80277
    Tel: 303-989-5356

Los Angeles Alliance of Charter Schools
    116 E. Martin Luther King Boulevard
    Los Angeles, CA 90011
    Tel: 213-235-6343; Fax: 213-235-6346

Massachusetts Charter School Association
    2602 Jackson Road
    Devens, MA 01432
    Tel: 508-635-1800; Fax: 508-635-1804

Michigan Association of Public School Academies (MAPSA)
    750 Michigan National Tower
    Lansing, MI 48933
    Tel: 517-374-9167; Fax: 517-374-9197

Minnesota Association of Charter Schools (MACS)
      Edvisions, 115 N. Main
      LeSueur, MN 56058
      Tel: 612-298-4624; Fax: 612-298-5756

Wisconsin Charter School Association
      2700 W. College Avenue
      Appleton, WI 54914
      Tel: 414-830-3560; Fax: 414-733-1802

Newsletters

CANECConnections.
      Available from:
      CANEC
      751 Laurel St., Box 414
      San Carlos, CA 94070-3122
      Tel: 415-598-8192; Fax: 415-591-1043

Charter School Newsletter.
      Available from:
      Charter School Resource Center
      Pioneer Institute for Public Policy Research
      85 Devonshire Street, 8th Floor
      Boston, MA 02109
      Tel: 617-723-2277; Fax: 617-723-1880

Charter School Resource Center Newsletter.
      Available from:
      Charter School Resource Center of New Jersey
      109 Church Street
      New Brunswick, NJ 08901
      Tel: 732-296-8379; Fax: 732-296-8380

Education Alert.
      Available from:
      Citizen Alliance for Choice in Education
      Box 767
      Acton, MA 01720
      Tel: 508-635-1800; Fax: 508-635-1804

FOCUS Newsletter.
Available from:
Friends of Choice in Urban Schools (FOCUS)
1530 16th Street, NW, Suite 001
Washington, DC 20036
Tel: 202-387-0405; Fax: 202-667-3798

New Hampshire Charter School Resource Center Newsletter.
Available from
New Hampshire Charter School Resource Center
c/o Josiah Bartlett, Center for Public Policy
P.O. Box 90
Hanover, NH 03755
or
P.O. Box 7897
Concord, NH 03301
Tel: 603-643-6115; Fax: 603-643-6476

Wisconsin Charter School Association Newsletter.
Available from:
Wisconsin Charter School Association
2700 W. College Avenue
Appleton, WI 54914
Tel: 414-830-3560; Fax: 414-733-1802

Parents

Becker, Henry J., Kathryn Nakagawa, and Ronald G. Corwin. *Parent Involvement Contracts in California's Charter Schools: Strategy for Educational Improvement or Method of Exclusion? April 1995.* Los Alamitos, Calif.: Southwest Regional Laboratory, 1995.

A look at the use of parent contracts in California charter schools that focuses on their implications for parent involvement and student selection.
Available from:
Southwest Regional Laboratory
4665 Lampson Avenue
Los Alamitos, CA 90720
Tel: 310-598-7661; Fax: 310-985-9635

Technical Assistance

Charter Foundation
    1045 SE Sixth Avenue
    Fort Lauderdale, FL 33044
    Tel: 954-564-2221; Fax: 954-564-2142

Charter School Assistance Center, The Center for Education Reform
    1001 Connecticut Avenue, NW, Suite 204
    Washington, DC 20036
    Tel: 800-521-2118; Fax: 202-822-5077

Charter School Resource Center, Pioneer Institute for Public Policy Research
    85 Devonshire Street, 8th Floor
    Boston, MA 02109
    Tel: 617-723-2277; Fax: 617-723-1880

Charter School Resource Center of New Jersey
    109 Church Street
    New Brunswick, NJ 08901
    Tel: 732-296-8379; Fax: 732-296-8380

Charter School Resource Center of Texas
    P. O. Box 782085
    San Antonio, TX 78278
    Tel: 210-408-7890; Fax: 210-408-1263

Charter School Strategies, Inc.
    210 West Grant Street, Suite 321
    Minneapolis, MN 55403
    Tel: 612-321-9221

Charter Schools Project
    California State University Institute for Education Reform
    6000 J Street
    Sacramento, CA 95819-6018
    Tel: 916-278-4600

Charter Schools Project
    Dusquesne University
    712 Rockwell Hall
    600 Forbes Avenue
    Pittsburgh, PA 15282
    Tel: 412-396-4492; Fax: 412-396-6175

Citizen Alliance for Choice in Education
Box 767
Acton, MA 01720
Tel: 508-635-1800; Fax: 508-635-1804

DC Committee on Public Education (COPE)
1155 15th Street, NW, Suite 301
Washington, DC 20005
Tel: 202-835-9011; Fax: 202-659-8621

Designs for Learning
1355 Pierce Butler
St. Paul, MN 55104
Tel: 612-645-0200; Fax: 612-645-0240

Drexel/Foundations Technical Assistance Center
32nd and Chestnut
Philadelphia, PA 19104
Tel: 215-895-2568; Fax: 215-895-5879

Friends of Choice in Urban Schools (FOCUS)
1530 16th Street, NW, Suite 001
Washington, DC 20036
Tel: 202-387-0405; Fax: 202-667-3798

Leadership for Quality Education (LQE)
One First National Plaza, Suite 3120
Chicago, IL 60603-2006
Tel: 312-853-1206; Fax: 312-853-1214

Leona Group LLC
4660 South Hagadorn Road, Suite 500
East Lansing, MI 48823
Tel: 517-333-9030; Fax: 517-333-4559

Michigan Resource Center for Charter Schools
Central Michigan University
Ronan Hall 220A
Mt. Pleasant, MI 48859
Tel: 517-774-2590; Fax: 517-774-2591

New Hampshire Charter School Resource Center
   c/o Josiah Bartlett, Center for Public Policy
   P.O. Box 90
   Hanover, NH 03755
   or
   P.O. Box 897
   Concord, NH 03301
   Tel: 603-643-6115; Fax: 603-643-6476

North Carolina Charter School Resource Center
   4711 Hope Valley Road, Suite 321
   Durham, NC 27707
   Tel: 919-682-1500 or 888-461-8824; Fax: 919-682-4320

Wisconsin Charter School Resource Center
   Marquette University, Institute for the Transformation of Learning
   Schroeder Health Complex, 146
   P.O. Box 1881
   Milwaukee, WI 53201-1881
   Tel: 414-288-3434; Fax: 414-288-6199

INDEX

RED

John Logan

RED

OBERON BOOKS
LONDON

Published in 2009 by Oberon Books Ltd
521 Caledonian Road, London N7 9RH
Tel: 020 7607 3637 / Fax: 020 7607 3629
e-mail: info@oberonbooks.com
www.oberonbooks.com

Reprinted 2010, 2011

A catalogue record for this book is available from the British
Library.

ISBN: 978-1-84002-944-4

Cover design by SpotCo

Printed in the USA, McNaughton&Gunn inc, ltd. Michigan

MAY

}
}

2011

Red was first performed at Donmar Warehouse, London on 3 December 2009, with the following cast:

ROTHKO, Alfred Molina
KEN, Eddie Redmayne

Director Michael Grandage
Designer Christopher Oram
Lighting Designer Neil Austin
Composer and Sound Designer Adam Cork

Red was first performed on Broadway at Golden Theatre, New York on 11 March 2010, with the following cast:

ROTHKO, Alfred Molina
KEN, Eddie Redmayne
ROTHKO UNDERSTUDY, Stephen Rowe
KEN UNDERSTUDY, Gabriel Ebert

Director Michael Grandage
Set and Costume Designer Christopher Oram
Lighting Designer Neil Austin
Composer and Sound Designer Adam Cork

New York Producers
Arielle Tepper Madover
Stephanie P. McClelland
Matthew Byam Shaw
Neal Street
Fox Theatricals
Ruth Hendel/Barbara Whitman
Philip Hagemann/Murray Rosenthal
The Donmar Warehouse

Characters

MARK ROTHKO
American painter, 50s or older

KEN
His new assistant, 20s

Setting

Rothko's studio, 222 Bowery, New York City.
Circa 1958-1959.

Rothko's studio is an old gymnasium. The hardwood floor is splattered and stained with hues of dark red paint. There is a cluttered counter or tables filled with buckets of paint, tins of turpentine, tubes of glue, crates of eggs, bottles of Scotch, packets of pigment, coffee cans filled with brushes, a portable burner or stovetop, and a phone. There is also a phonograph with messy stacks of records.

There is one door leading to an unseen vestibule where the characters change into their work clothes and enter and exit the studio.

Most importantly, representations of some of Rothko's magnificent Seagram Mural paintings are stacked and displayed around the room. Rothko had a pulley system that could raise, lower and display several of the paintings simultaneously. The paintings could be repositioned throughout the play, with a different arrangement for each scene.

There is also an imaginary painting 'hanging' right in front of the audience, which Rothko studies throughout the play.

Alternately, the entire setting could be abstract.

Dedicated to Stephen Sondheim

For reminding me

SCENE ONE

ROTHKO stands, staring forward.

He is looking directly at the audience. (He is actually studying one of his Seagram Mural paintings, which hangs before him.)

Pause.

ROTHKO lights a cigarette. He wears thick glasses and old, ill-fitting clothes spattered with specks of glue and paint.

Contemplative classical music is playing on a phonograph.

ROTHKO takes a drag on his cigarette.

Pause.

There is the sound of a door opening and closing from the unseen entry vestibule offstage.

KEN, a man in his early 20s, enters nervously. He wears a suit and tie. This is the first time he has been in the studio. He looks around.

He is about to speak.

ROTHKO gestures for him not to speak. Then he beckons for KEN to join him.

KEN goes to ROTHKO, stands next to him.

ROTHKO indicates the central painting; the audience.

ROTHKO: What do you see?

KEN is about to respond –

ROTHKO: Wait. Stand closer. You've got to get close. Let it pulsate. Let it work on you. Closer. Too close. There. Let it spread out. Let it wrap its arms around you; let it *embrace* you, filling even your peripheral vision so nothing else exists or has ever existed or will ever exist. Let the picture do its work – But work with it. Meet it halfway for God's sake! Lean forward, lean into it. Engage with it!… Now, what do you see? – Wait, wait, wait!

He hurries and lowers the lighting a bit, then returns to KEN.

ROTHKO: So, now, what do you see? – Be specific. No, be exact. Be exact – but sensitive. You understand? Be kind. Be a human being, that's all I can say. Be a *human being* for once in your life! These pictures deserve compassion and they live or die in the eye of the sensitive viewer, they quicken only if the empathetic viewer will let them. That is what they cry out for. That is why they where created. That is what they deserve... Now... What do you see?

Beat.

KEN: Red.

ROTHKO: But do you *like* it?

KEN: Mm.

ROTHKO: Speak up.

KEN: Yes.

ROTHKO: Of course you *like* it – how can you not *like* it?! Everyone likes everything nowadays. They like the television and the phonograph and the soda pop and the shampoo and the Cracker Jack. Everything becomes everything else and it's all nice and pretty and *likable*. Everything is fun in the sun! Where's the discernment? Where's the arbitration that separates what I *like* from what I *respect*, what I deem *worthy*, what has...listen to me now...*significance*.

ROTHKO moves and turns up the lights again, although he keeps them relatively low, and then switches off the record player, as he continues.

ROTHKO: Maybe this is a dinosaur talking. Maybe I'm a dinosaur sucking up the oxygen from you cunning little mammals hiding in the bushes waiting to take over. Maybe I'm speaking a lost language unknown to your generation. But a generation that does not aspire to seriousness, to meaning, is unworthy to walk in the shadow of those who have gone before, I mean those who have struggled and surmounted, I mean those who have aspired, I mean Rembrandt, I mean Turner, I mean Michelangelo and Matisse… I mean obviously Rothko.

He stares at KEN, challenging.

ROTHKO: Do you aspire?

KEN: Yes.

ROTHKO: To what? To what do you aspire?

KEN: I want to be a painter so I guess I aspire to…painting.

ROTHKO: Then those clothes won't do. We work here. Hang up your jacket outside. I appreciate you put on your Sunday clothes to impress me, it's poignant really, touches me, but it's ridiculous. We work hard here; this isn't a goddamn Old World salon with tea cakes and lemonade. Go hang up your jacket outside.

KEN exits to the entry vestibule off stage. He returns without his jacket. Takes off his tie and rolls up his sleeves.

ROTHKO: Sidney told you what I need here?

KEN: Yes.

ROTHKO busies himself, sorting brushes, arranging canvases, etc., as:

ROTHKO: We start every morning at nine and work until five. Just like bankers. You'll help me stretch the canvases and mix the paints and clean the brushes and build the stretchers and move the paintings and also help apply the ground color – which is *not* painting, so any lunatic assumptions you make in that direction you need to banish immediately. You'll pick up food and cigarettes and anything else I want, any whim, no matter how demanding or demeaning. If you don't like that, leave right now. Answer me. Yes or no.

KEN: Yes.

ROTHKO: Consider: I am not your rabbi, I am not your father, I am not your shrink, I am not your friend, I am not your teacher – I am your employer. You understand?

KEN: Yes.

ROTHKO: As my assistant you will see many things here, many ingenious things. But they're all secret. You cannot talk about any of this. Don't think I don't have enemies because I do and I don't just mean the other painters and gallery owners and museum curators and goddamn-son-of-a-bitch-art-critics, not to mention that vast panoply of disgruntled viewers who loathe me and my work because they do not have the heart, nor the patience, nor the capacity, to think, to *understand*, because they are not *human beings*, like we talked about, you remember?

KEN: Yes.

ROTHKO: I'm painting a series of murals now – (*He gestures all around.*) – I'll probably do thirty or forty and then choose which work best, in concert, like a fugue. You'll help me put on the undercoat and then I'll paint them and then I'll look at them and then paint some more. I do a lot of layers, one after another, like a glaze, slowly building the image, like pentimento, letting the luminescence emerge until it's done.

KEN: How do you know when it's done?

ROTHKO: There's tragedy in every brush stroke.

KEN: Ah.

ROTHKO: Swell. Let's have a drink.

ROTHKO pours two glasses of Scotch. He hands one to KEN.

They drink. KEN is unused to drinking so early in the morning.

Beat.

ROTHKO stares at him, appraising.

ROTHKO: Answer me a question… Don't think about it, just say the first thing that comes into your head. No cognition.

KEN: Okay.

ROTHKO: You ready?

KEN: Yeah.

ROTHKO: Who's your favourite painter?

KEN: Jackson Pollock.

ROTHKO: (*Wounded.*) Ah.

KEN: Sorry.

ROTHKO: No, no –

KEN: Let me do it again.

ROTHKO: No –

KEN: Come on –

ROTHKO: No, it's silly –

KEN: Come on, ask me again.

ROTHKO: Who's your favourite painter?

KEN: Picasso.

> *KEN laughs.*
>
> *ROTHKO doesn't.*
>
> *ROTHKO glowers at him.*
>
> *KEN's laugh dies.*
>
> *ROTHKO roams.*

ROTHKO: Hmm, Pollock… Always Pollock. Don't get me wrong, he was a great painter, we came up together, I knew him very well.

KEN: What was he like?

ROTHKO: You read Nietzsche?

KEN: What?

ROTHKO: You ever read Nietzsche? *The Birth of Tragedy*?

KEN: No.

ROTHKO: You call yourself an artist? One can't discuss Pollock without it. One can't discuss anything without it. What do they teach you in art school now?

KEN: I –

ROTHKO: You ever read Freud?

KEN: No –

ROTHKO: Jung?

KEN: Well –

ROTHKO: Byron? Wordsworth? Aeschylus? Turgenev? Sophocles? Schopenhauer? Shakespeare? *Hamlet*? At least *Hamlet*, please God! Quote me *Hamlet*. Right now.

KEN: 'To be or not to be, that is the question.'

ROTHKO: Is that the question?

KEN: I don't know.

ROTHKO: You have a lot to learn, young man. Philosophy. Theology. Literature. Poetry. Drama. History. Archeology. Anthropology. Mythology. Music. These are your tools as much as brush and pigment. You cannot be an *artist* until you are civilized. You cannot be *civilized* until you learn. To be civilized is to know where you belong in the continuum of your art and your world. To surmount the past, you must know the past.

KEN: I thought you weren't my teacher.

ROTHKO: You should be so blessed I talk to you about art.

ROTHKO moves away.

Beat.

ROTHKO: How do you feel?

KEN: How do I feel?

ROTHKO indicates the huge mural paintings all around them.

ROTHKO: How do *they* make you feel?

KEN: Give me a second.

KEN moves to the middle of the room and takes in all the paintings.

ROTHKO: So?

KEN: Give me a second.

Beat.

KEN: Disquieted.

ROTHKO: And?

KEN: Thoughtful.

ROTHKO: And?

KEN: Um… Sad.

ROTHKO: *Tragic.*

KEN: Yeah.

ROTHKO: They're for a restaurant.

KEN: What?

ROTHKO: They're for a restaurant.

ROTHKO smiles. He enjoys this.

ROTHKO: So I'm minding my own business when Mister Philip Johnson calls me. You know Mister Philip Johnson, the world-renowned architect?

KEN: Not personally.

ROTHKO: Of course you don't know him personally, you don't know anyone personally. Don't interrupt. Mister Philip Johnson calls me. He's designing the new Seagram Building on Park Avenue, he and Mies van der Rohe. These are names with which to conjure, are they not? Philip Johnson and Mies van der Rohe, titans of their field, revolutionists. Together they are making a building unlike anything the world has yet seen, reflecting the golden ambitions of not only this city and its inhabitants but of all mankind. In this building there is to be a restaurant called the Four Seasons, like the Vivaldi, and on the walls of this restaurant.

He gestures expansively to his paintings.

Beat.

ROTHKO: (*Proud.*) Thirty-five thousand dollars they are paying me. No other painter comes close.

KEN is impressed. Thirty-five thousand dollars is a fortune. Call it two million dollars in today's money.

ROTHKO walks to the center of the room, filling himself with the work.

ROTHKO: My first murals… Imagine a frieze all around the room, a continuous narrative filling the walls, one to another, each a new chapter, the story unfolding, look and they are there, inescapable and inexorable, like doom.

KEN: Are these ones done?

ROTHKO: They're in process. I have to study them now.

KEN: Study them?

ROTHKO: Most of painting is thinking. Didn't they teach you that? Ten percent is putting paint onto the canvas. The rest is waiting.

ROTHKO takes in his paintings.

ROTHKO: All my life I wanted just this, my friend: to create a *place*... A place where the viewer could live in contemplation with the work and give it some of the same attention and care I gave it. Like a chapel... A place of communion.

KEN: But...it's a restaurant.

ROTHKO: No... I will make it a temple.

Beat.

ROTHKO is lost in his paintings.

KEN watches him for a moment.

Then he moves to the phonograph. He turns it on, lowers the needle. The classical music plays.

He studies ROTHKO.

SCENE TWO

ROTHKO stands starting at the central painting; the audience.

Classical music plays from the phonograph. (ROTHKO favoured Mozart and Schubert.)

KEN enters. He carries bags of Chinese takeout food. He now wears work clothes splattered with paint and glue. Months have passed and he is more comfortable here.

KEN puts a handful of change into an empty coffee can and then unloads the cartons of food.

ROTHKO muses.

ROTHKO: Rembrandt and Rothko... Rembrandt and Rothko... Rothko and Rembrandt... Rothko and Rembrandt... And Turner. Rothko and Rembrandt and Turner... Rothko and Rembrandt and Turner –

KEN: – Oh my.

Beat.

ROTHKO lights a cigarette.

KEN: The Chinese place is closing.

ROTHKO: Everything worthwhile ends. We are in the perpetual process now: creation, maturation, cessation.

KEN: There's another Chinese round the corner.

ROTHKO: The eternal cycles grind on, generations pass away, hope turns arid, but there's another Chinese round the corner.

KEN: Not much for small talk.

ROTHKO: It's small.

He joins KEN. He stands and eats Chinese food messily with a fork through the following.

KEN: I went to the Modern last night, saw the Picasso show.

ROTHKO: And?

KEN: I don't think he's so much concerned with generations passing away.

ROTHKO: Don't kid yourself, kid. That man – though now a charlatan of course signing menus for money like Dali, when he's not making ugly little pots, also for money – that man at his best understood the workings of time… Where's the receipt?

KEN gives him the receipt for the Chinese food.

ROTHKO puts it into a shoebox filled with other receipts as he continues without stopping.

ROTHKO: Tragic, really, to grow superfluous in your own lifetime. We destroyed Cubism, de Kooning and me and Pollock and Barnett Newman and all the others. We stomped it to death. Nobody can paint a Cubist picture today.

KEN: You take pride in that. 'Stomping' Cubism to death.

ROTHKO: The child must banish the father. Respect him, but kill him.

KEN: And enjoy it?

ROTHKO: Doesn't matter. Just be audacious and do it…
Courage in painting isn't facing the blank canvas, it's facing Manet, it's facing Velasquez. All we can do is move beyond what was there, to what is here, and hope to get some intimation of what will be here. 'What is past and passing and to come.' That's Yeats, whom you haven't read.

KEN: Come on, but Picasso –

ROTHKO tries another carton of food, keeps eating.

ROTHKO: Picasso I thank for teaching me that movement is everything! Movement is life. The second we're born we squall, we writhe, we squirm; to live is to move. Without movement paintings are what?

KEN: Dead?

ROTHKO: Precisely… (*He gestures to his paintings.*) Look at the *tension* between the blocks of color: the dark and the light, the red and the black and the brown. They exist in a state of flux – of movement. They abut each other on the actual canvas, so too do they abut each other in your eye. They ebb and flow and shift, gently pulsating. The more you look at them the more they move… They float in space, they breathe… Movement, communication, gesture, flux, interaction; letting them work… They're not dead because they're not static. They move through space if you let them, this movement takes time, so they're temporal. They require *time.*

KEN: They demand it. They don't work without it.

ROTHKO: This is why it's so important to me to create a *place*. A place the viewer can contemplate the paintings over time and let them move.

KEN: (*Excited.*) They *need* the viewer. They're not like representational pictures, like traditional landscapes or portraits.

ROTHKO: Tell me why.

KEN: Because they *change*, they move, they pulse. Representational pictures are unchanging; they don't require the active participation of the viewer. Go to the Louvre in the middle of the night and the 'Mona Lisa' will still be smiling. But do these paintings still pulse when they're alone?

KEN is lost in thought.

ROTHKO watches him, pleased.

KEN: That's why you keep the lights so low.

ROTHKO: Is it?

KEN: To help the illusion. Like a magician. Like a play. To keep it mysterious, to let the pictures pulsate. Turn on bright lights and the stage effect is ruined – suddenly it's nothing but a bare stage with a bunch of fake walls.

KEN goes to the light switches. He snaps on all the lights. Ugly fluorescent lights sizzle on. The room immediately loses its magic.

ROTHKO: What do you see?

KEN: My eyes are adjusting… Just… White.

ROTHKO: What does white make you think of?

KEN: Bones, skeletons… Charnel house… Anemia… Cruelty.

ROTHKO is surprised by this response.

ROTHKO: Really?

KEN: It's like an operating theatre now.

ROTHKO: How does white make you *feel?*

KEN: Frightened?

ROTHKO: Why?

KEN: Doesn't matter.

ROTHKO: Why?

KEN: It's like the snow...outside the room where my parents died. It was winter. I remember the snow outside the window: white... (*Turns his attention to the paintings.*) And the pictures in this light... They're flat. Vulgar... This light hurts them.

ROTHKO turns off the fluorescent lights.

The normal light returns.

ROTHKO: You see how it is with them? How vulnerable they are?... People think I'm controlling: controlling the light; controlling the height of the pictures; controlling the shape of the gallery... It's not controlling, it's *protecting.* A picture lives by companionship. It dies by the same token. It's a risky act to send it out into the world.

KEN tosses away the cartons of food and straightens up.

ROTHKO puts on a new classical record. Moves back to studying his central painting.

A beat as the mood settles.

KEN: You ever paint outdoors?

ROTHKO: You mean out in nature?

KEN: Yeah.

ROTHKO: Nature doesn't work for me. The light's no good.

KEN is amused.

ROTHKO: All those bugs – ach! I know, those *plein air* painters, they sing to you endless paeans about the majesty of natural sunlight. Get out there and muck around in the grass, they tell you, like a cow. When I was young I didn't know any better so I would haul my supplies out there and the wind would blow the paper and the easel would fall over and the ants would get in the paint. Oy… But then I go to Rome for the first time. I go to the Santa Maria del Popolo to see Caravaggio's 'Conversion of Saul,' which turns out is tucked away in a dark corner of this dark church with no natural light. It's like a cave. But the painting *glowed!* With a sort of *rapture* it glowed. Consider: Caravaggio was commissioned to paint the picture for this specific place, he had no choice. He stands there and he looks around. It's like under the ocean it's so goddamn dark. How's he going to paint here? He turns to his creator: 'God, help me, unworthy sinner that I am. Tell me, O Lord on High, what the fuck do I do now?!'

KEN laughs.

ROTHKO: Then it comes to him: the divine spark. He illuminates the picture from *within*! He gives it *inner* luminosity. It *lives…* Like one of those bioluminescent fish from the bottom of the ocean, radiating its own effulgence. You understand? Caravaggio was –

He abruptly stops.

KEN looks at him.

Beat.

ROTHKO stares at his painting.

He tilts his head.

Like he's listening.

Like he's seeing something new in the painting.

ROTHKO: Bring me the second bucket.

KEN, excited, brings him a brush and a bucket of dark, maroon paint.

KEN: Are you really going to paint?

ROTHKO: What the hell do you think I *have* been doing?!

KEN retreats.

He watches ROTHKO closely.

ROTHKO dips the five-inch housepainter's brush into the paint.

He's ready.

Then he stands there, frozen.

Just his eyes move craftily over the canvas.

Paint drips.

KEN is breathless.

ROTHKO is coiled.

He tilts his head, studying, adjudicating.

He considers the color of the paint in the bucket. Needs something.

ROTHKO: Gimme black number four and the first maroon.

KEN brings some powdered pigments in old jars.

ROTHKO instructs, still barely moving. His eyes dart from the bucket of paint to the canvas.

ROTHKO: A pinch of black.

KEN adds a bit of black pigment, stirs it carefully.

ROTHKO: Just that amount again.

KEN adds a bit more, keeps stirring.

ROTHKO: Twice as much maroon.

KEN adds some maroon pigment, keeps stirring.

ROTHKO is unsure.

He looks at the painting.

The moment is passing.

He is getting desperate.

ROTHKO: (*To himself, frustrated.*) Come on…come on…come on… What does it need?

KEN: Red.

ROTHKO: I wasn't talking to you!

Beat.

Tragically, the moment has passed for ROTHKO.

He FLINGS the paintbrush away. It splatters.

He spins on KEN.

ROTHKO: DON'T YOU EVER DO THAT AGAIN!

He rages, stomping restlessly around the room.

ROTHKO: By what right do you speak?! By what right do you express an opinion on my work? Who the fuck are you? What have you done? What have you seen? Where have you earned the right to exist here with me and these things you don't understand?! 'RED?!' You want to paint the thing?! Go ahead – here's red–!

He clumsily slings packets of various red paints at KEN.

ROTHKO: And red! And red! And red! – I don't even know what that means! What does 'red' mean to me? You mean scarlet? You mean crimson? You mean plum-mulberry-magenta-burgundy-salmon-carmine-carnelian-coral? Anything but 'red!' What is 'RED?!'

ROTHKO stands, getting his breath, collecting himself.

Beat.

KEN picks up the packets of paint from the floor.

ROTHKO prowls, discontent.

Pause.

KEN: I meant sunrise.

ROTHKO: Sunrise?

KEN: I meant the red at sunrise… The feeling of it.

ROTHKO: (*Derisive.*) Oh, the 'feeling of it.'

Beat.

KEN continues to clean up, clearing away the bucket of paint and brush.

Beat.

ROTHKO: What do you mean the feeling of it?

KEN: I didn't mean red paint only. I meant the *emotion* of red at sunrise.

ROTHKO: Sunrise isn't red.

KEN: Yes it is.

ROTHKO: I'm telling you it's not.

KEN: Sunrise is red and red is sunrise.

KEN keeps cleaning up.

KEN: Red is heart beat. Red is passion. Red wine. Red roses. Red lipstick. Beets. Tulips. Peppers.

ROTHKO: Arterial blood.

KEN: That too.

ROTHKO thinks about it.

ROTHKO: Rust on the bike on the lawn.

KEN: And apples… And tomatoes.

ROTHKO: Dresden firestorm at night. The sun in Rousseau, the flag in Delacroix, the robe in El Greco.

KEN: A rabbit's nose. An albino's eyes. A parakeet.

ROTHKO: Florentine marble. Atomic flash. Nick yourself shaving, blood in the Barbasol.

KEN: The Ruby Slippers. Technicolor. That phone to the Kremlin on the President's desk.

ROTHKO: Russian flag, Nazi flag, Chinese flag.

KEN: Persimmons. Pomegranates. Red Light District. Red tape. Rouge.

ROTHKO: Lava. Lobsters. Scorpions.

KEN: Stop sign. Sports car. A blush.

ROTHKO: Viscera. Flame. Dead Fauvists.

KEN: Traffic lights. Titian hair.

ROTHKO: Slash your wrists. Blood in the sink.

KEN: Santa Claus.

ROTHKO: Satan.

Beat.

ROTHKO: So…red.

KEN: Exactly.

ROTHKO gazes thoughtfully at his painting.

ROTHKO: We got more cigarettes?

KEN gets a pack of cigarettes from a drawer and tosses them to ROTHKO.

ROTHKO opens them and lights one as:

ROTHKO: More than anything, you know what?

KEN: What?

ROTHKO: Matisse's painting 'The Red Studio.' It's a picture of his own studio; the walls are a brilliant red, the floor and furniture, all red, like the color had radiated out of him and swallowed everything up. When the Modern first put that picture up I would spend hours looking at it. Day after day I would go… You could argue that everything I do today, you can trace the bloodlines back to that painting and those hours standing there, letting the painting work, allowing it to *move*… The more I looked at it the more it pulsated around me, I was totally saturated, it swallowed me… Such *plains* of red he made, such energetic blocks of color, such emotion!

Beat.

ROTHKO sits in an old arm chair, staring at the central painting. Exhausted and depressed.

KEN senses the change in ROTHKO's mood.

ROTHKO takes off his thick glasses, cleans them on his shirt as:

ROTHKO: That was a long time ago.

KEN: It's still there.

ROTHKO: I can't look at it now.

KEN: Why?

ROTHKO: It's too depressing.

KEN: How can all that red be depressing?

ROTHKO: I don't see the red any more… Even in that painting, that total and profound emersion in red…it's there. The mantel above a dresser, just over the centerline, set off by yellow of all goddamn things. He wanted it inescapable.

KEN: What?

ROTHKO: Black.

KEN: The color black?

ROTHKO: The thing black.

Beat.

ROTHKO: There is only one thing I fear in life, my friend…
One day the black will swallow the red.

He puts on his glasses again and stares at his painting.

SCENE THREE

KEN is alone. He is at a stove or burner, gently heating and stirring liquid in a large pot. This mixture will be the base layer for a new blank canvas.

A small painting, wrapped in brown paper, is tucked unobtrusively in a corner.

He talks on the phone as he stirs.

KEN: (*On phone.*) …that's easy for you to say, you don't know him… (*He glances to the wrapped painting.*) … I'll show it to him if I think the moment's right. He knows I'm a painter, he's got to be expecting it… No, no it depends on his mood … don't tell me what to do! You're just like him…

He hears the sounds of ROTHKO entering outside.

KEN: He's here. I'll tell you how it goes. Pray for me.

He hangs up.

ROTHKO enters with some supplies for the base layer. He does not notice the wrapped painting.

KEN: Good morning.

ROTHKO: Morning. I got the other maroon… I'll take over, you finish the canvas.

ROTHKO goes to the pot and takes over stirring. He adds some new maroon pigment to the mixture. Like concocting a witch's brew, he also stirs in glue, chemicals, chalk, raw eggs and other powdered pigments.

KEN works on tightening and stapling a blank canvas. It is square, about six feet by six feet or larger.

ROTHKO: I went by the Seagram building last night, it's coming along.

KEN: How's the restaurant?

ROTHKO: Still under construction, but they took me around, got a sense of it.

KEN: And?

ROTHKO: Too much natural light, as always, but it'll work. You'll be able to see the murals from the main dining room... I made some sketches; I'll find them for you.

KEN: You ever worry it's not the right place for them?

ROTHKO: How can it not be the right place for them when they are being created specifically for that place? Sometimes your logic baffles me.

ROTHKO goes to the phonograph and flips through the records.

KEN glances again to his wrapped painting. Is this the time to bring it up? No. He doesn't have the nerve quite yet.

ROTHKO picks a classical record and puts it on.

Then he returns to stirring the mixture.

Beat.

KEN: So I read Nietzsche. *Birth of Tragedy* like you said.

ROTHKO: Like I said?

KEN: You said if I wanted to know about Jackson Pollock I had to read *The Birth of Tragedy.*

ROTHKO: I said that?

KEN: Yeah.

ROTHKO: I don't remember. It's very like something I would say.

KEN: So what about Pollock?

ROTHKO: First tell me what you make of the book.

KEN: Interesting.

ROTHKO: That's like saying 'red.' Don't be enigmatic; you're too young to be enigmatic.

KEN: I think I know why you wanted me to read it.

ROTHKO: Why?

KEN: Because you see yourself as Apollo and you see him as Dionysus.

ROTHKO: Don't be so pedestrian. Think more.

ROTHKO adds turpentine to the mixture, checks the consistency by letting it run off his paint stirrer. He wants it thin, like a glaze.

KEN stops working.

KEN: Dionysus is the God of wine and excess; of movement and transformation. This is Pollock: wild; rebellious; drunken and unrestrained. The raw experience itself… Apollo is the God of order, method and boundaries. This is Rothko: intellectual; rabbinical; sober and restrained. The raw experience leavened by contemplation… He splatters paint. You study it… He's Dionysus and you're Apollo.

ROTHKO: Exactly right but for entirely missing the point.

KEN: How so?

ROTHKO: You miss the tragedy. The point is always the tragedy.

KEN: For you.

ROTHKO: You think human beings can be divided up so neatly into character types? You think the multifarious complexities and nuances of the psyche – evolving through countless generations, perverted and demented through social neurosis and personal anguish, moulded by faith and lack of faith – can really be so goddamn simple? Pollock is Emotion and Rothko is Intellect? You embarrass yourself… Think more.

KEN thinks as he continues to work on the canvas.

ROTHKO continues to stir the paint, occasionally glancing at KEN.

KEN stops.

KEN: Maybe it's like one of your paintings.

ROTHKO: Most things are. How?

KEN: Dark and light, order and chaos, existing at the same time in the same plain, pulsing back and forth… We pulse too; we're subjects of both Apollo *and* Dionysus, not one or the other. We ebb and flow, like the colors in your pictures, the ecstasy of the Dionysian at war with the restraint of the Apollonian.

ROTHKO: Not at war.

KEN: Not at war?

ROTHKO: It's not really conflict. More like symbiosis.

KEN: They need each other. Dionysus' passion is focused – is made bearable – by Apollo's will to form. In fact the only way we can *endure* the sheer ferocity of Dionysus' emotion is because we have the control and intelligence of Apollo, otherwise the emotion would overwhelm us… So back and forth we go, myth to myth, pulsating.

ROTHKO: And the perfect life would be perfectly balanced between the two, everlastingly on the fulcrum. But our *tragedy* is that we can never achieve that balance. We exist – all of us, for all time – in a state of perpetual dissonance… We long for the raw truth of emotion, but can only endure it with the cool lie of reason… We seek to capture the ephemeral, the miraculous, and put it onto canvas, stopping time but, like an entomologist pinning a butterfly, it dies when we try…. We're foolish that way, we human beings… We try to make the red black.

KEN: But the black is always there, like the mantle in Matisse.

ROTHKO: Like the snow outside the window. It never goes away. Once glimpsed, we can't help being preoccupied with it for the intimations of our mortality are… (*He gestures: everywhere.*) … But still we go on, clinging to that tiny bit of hope – that red – that makes the rest endurable.

KEN: Or just less unendurable.

ROTHKO: That's my friend Jackson Pollock. Finally it was just unendurable.

KEN: What do you mean?

ROTHKO: His suicide.

KEN: He didn't commit suicide.

ROTHKO: Didn't he?

KEN thinks about this as he continues to tighten the canvas.

ROTHKO isn't satisfied with the music. He puts on a different classical record. He listens for a moment and then returns to stirring the mixture.

KEN: Jackson Pollock died in a car accident.

ROTHKO: A man spends years getting drunk, day after day, hammered. Then he gets into an Oldsmobile convertible and races around these little country roads like a lunatic. You tell me what that is if not a lazy suicide… Believe me, when I commit suicide there won't be any doubt about it. No mysterious crumpled car in a ditch, did he or didn't he, it gives me a headache it's so boring.

KEN: 'When' you commit suicide?

ROTHKO: What?

KEN: You said 'When I commit suicide.'

ROTHKO: No I didn't.

KEN: You did.

ROTHKO: You misheard... Let me tell you one thing about your hero, that man really confronted his tragedy. He was valiant in the face of it, he endured as long as he could, then he tried to recede from life, but how could he? He was Jackson Pollock.

KEN: What was his tragedy?

ROTHKO: He became famous.

KEN: Don't be glib.

ROTHKO: His muse evacuated. He grew tired of his form. He grew tired of himself. He lost faith in his viewers... Take your pick... He no longer believed there were any real human beings out there to look at pictures.

KEN: How does that happen to a man?

ROTHKO: Better you should ask how occasionally it doesn't happen.

KEN: I mean he's an artist, he's in *Life* magazine, he's young, he's famous, he has money –

ROTHKO: That's exactly it. Here's a schmuck from Wyoming who can paint. Suddenly he's a *commodity*. He's 'Jackson Pollock.' Lemme tell you, kid, that Oldsmobile convertible really did kill him. Not because it crashed, because it *existed*. Why the fuck did Jackson Pollock have an Oldsmobile convertible?

KEN: So artists should starve?

ROTHKO: Yes, artists should starve. Except me.

KEN smiles.

He has completed working on the canvas.

KEN: Take a look.

ROTHKO moves to the canvas, stands over it, carefully studying it, walking around it. He is looking for flaws in the canvas, as:

ROTHKO: You would have loved Jackson. He was a downtown guy, a real Bohemian. No banker's hours for him, believe you me. Every night the drinking and the talking and the fighting and the dancing and the staying up late; like everyone's romantic idea of what an artist ought to be: the anti-Rothko… At his worst you still loved him though; you loved him because he loved art so much… He thought it *mattered.* He thought painting mattered… Does not the poignancy stop your heart?… How could this story not end in tragedy?

Beat.

ROTHKO: Goya said, 'We have Art that we may not perish from Truth.'… Pollock saw some truth. Then he didn't have art to protect him any more… Who could survive that?

Beat.

ROTHKO emerges from his thoughts.

He nods to KEN.

They lift the canvas from the floor, lean it up against a sawhorse, easel or wall.

ROTHKO studies it minutely.

He delicately picks lint from the canvas. He gently blows remnants of dust away.

He continues to study the canvas as:

ROTHKO: I was walking up to my house last week and this couple was passing. Lady looks in the window, says: 'I wonder who owns all the Rothkos.'… Just like that I'm a noun. A Rothko.

KEN: A commodity.

ROTHKO: An overmantle.

KEN: A what?

ROTHKO continues to study the blank canvas for flaws, for discoloration, for imperfection. He moves closer, he backs all the way up, he moves closer again, tilting his head back and forth, adjudicating, as:

ROTHKO: The overmantles. Those paintings doomed to become *decoration.* You know, over the fireplace in the penthouse. They say to you, 'I need something to work with the sofa, you understand. Or something bright and cheery for the breakfast nook, which is orange, do you have anything in orange? Or burnt-umber? Or sea-foam green? Here's a paint chip from the Sherwin-Williams. And could you cut it down to fit the sideboard?'… Or even worse, 'Darling, I simply *must* have one because my neighbour has one, that social-climbing bitch, in fact if she has one, I need *three*!'… Or even worse, 'I must have one because the New York Times tells me I should have one – or someone told me the New York Times tells me I should have one because who has time to read any more.'… 'Oh, don't make me look at it! I never look at it! It's so depressing!'… 'All those fuzzy rectangles, my kid could do that in kindergarten, it's nothing but a scam, this guy's a fraud.'… Still, they buy it… It's an investment… It's screwing the neighbours… It's buying class… It's buying taste… It goes with the lamp… It's cheaper than a Pollock… It's interior decoration… It's anything but what it is.

Beat.

ROTHKO seems to have accepted the canvas.

ROTHKO: Okey-dokey. Let's prime the canvas.

They work together now.

They have done this many times, it is a well-practised ritual.

They pour the paint/glue mixture from the stove – the base layer for the canvas – into two large buckets. The mixture is a thin liquid, almost a glaze, of dark plum.

They bring the buckets to either side of the six-foot square canvas. They make sure the canvas is secure.

They prepare house painting brushes. ROTHKO rubs his rhythmically across his hand, warming and limbering the bristles.

KEN waits. Ready.

ROTHKO stares intently at the blank canvas.

A long beat as he rubs his brush back and forth across his hand, thinking.

KEN watches him, poised.

Then ROTHKO goes to the phonograph, flips through the stack of records, finds the one he wants, and puts it onto the phonograph.

He lowers the needle. He listens. He lifts the needle again. Finally finds the exact place in the record he is looking for. He lowers the needle.

Spirited classical music plays.

He returns to the canvas.

He nods to KEN.

Ready? Ready.

They dip their brushes.

They are on opposite sides of the canvas.

KEN crouches; he will do the lower half of the canvas.

ROTHKO stands tall; he will do the upper half of the canvas.

KEN waits for ROTHKO to begin.

ROTHKO waits for the music.

With theatrical panache, ROTHKO waits for the exact moment the music thunders most dramatically and then –

He begins to paint –

He moves very quickly –

Using strong, broad strokes he sweeps across the top of the canvas as quickly as possible – big, horizontal gestures – moving fast to make sure the base layer is even and smooth –

KEN does the same for the bottom half of the painting –

Some of ROTHKO's paint drips and splashes down on KEN –

It is like choreography, they move in sync, they move toward each other and then cross, ROTHKO lurching back awkwardly as he continues to paint so KEN can dive in under him gracefully as he continues to paint –

The thin, watery paint splatters and splashes as they dip their brushes and assault the canvas –

It is hard, fast, thrilling work –

The music swells –

And then they are done.

The white canvas is now an even, flat plain of dark plum.

ROTHKO steps back, exhausted, panting for air.

KEN sits heavily on the floor, also exhausted.

Beat.

ROTHKO lights a cigarette.

Then he turns off the phonograph.

KEN rises and cleans himself with a towel. Then he changes his paint-stained shirt.

He begins to straighten up: hauling the buckets away; wiping up the floor; cleaning the brushes.

ROTHKO minutely studies the now-primed canvas.

Then he steps back and back, studies the canvas from across the studio.

ROTHKO: (*Musing.*) So…so…so…it'll do… Maybe it'll do… Possibly adequate… What do you think?

KEN: You mean me? You want me to answer?

ROTHKO: Who else?

KEN: It's a…a good ground, a good base layer. Nice and even.

ROTHKO: We'll see when it dries. Then I can start to paint.

KEN: You really care what I think?

ROTHKO: Not at all.

KEN smiles, continues to clean up.

Then he stops abruptly.

Something about the freshly-primed canvas strikes him.

He stares at it.

Surprisingly, tears come to his eyes. The emotion is unexpected.

ROTHKO: What?

KEN: Nothing…

ROTHKO: What is it?

KEN: It's strange… I'm remembering something… The, um, color…is…

ROTHKO: What?

KEN: Doesn't matter.

ROTHKO: What?

KEN: Dried blood… When the blood dried it got *darker*. On the carpet.

ROTHKO: Which carpet?

KEN: Where my parents died.

KEN tries to shake off the thought. He moves away.

But then he stops again. He can't shake the emotion.

The canvas draws him back.

KEN: It's exactly the color. When the blood dried it got *darker*, that surprised me. I remember being surprised by that…

ROTHKO is intrigued.

ROTHKO: What happened to your parents?

KEN: I don't want to talk about it.

ROTHKO: Yes you do.

KEN: They were murdered.

ROTHKO: Did you say murdered?

KEN: Mm.

ROTHKO: How old were you?

KEN: Seven. This was back in Iowa.

ROTHKO: What happened?

KEN: I honestly don't remember it too well.

ROTHKO: Sure you do.

KEN stares forward, lost in thought.

Beat.

ROTHKO: What do you see?

KEN shakes his head.

ROTHKO: What do you see?

Beat.

KEN: (*Reliving it.*) I woke up…and the first thing I saw was the snow outside my window. I was glad it snowed because it was Saturday and I could go sledding. My Dad would take me sledding, me and my sister. But…but…I didn't smell anything. That was weird. Normally my Mom would be up making breakfast. It was really quiet. I put on my slippers – they were those Neolite ones that look like moccasins. Go into the hall… Now it's really quiet… And it's *cold.* There's a window open somewhere… Then I see my sister, she's just standing in the hallway, staring into my parent's room. The door's open. My sister…she's standing in a puddle of pee. Just staring. Her eyes… I go to the door and look in and see the snow first. Outside the window, so much snow, maybe I'll still go sledding. And then the blood. The bed's stained with it. And the wall. They're on the bed… It was a knife… Apparently it was a knife, I found out later.

Beat.

KEN: Burglars, I found out. At least two of them… But right now I don't know what to do. I just *see*… I… Don't want my sister to see any more. My little sister… I turn around and push her out and shut the door. The door handle… With blood… Is red.

Beat.

KEN: That's all.

ROTHKO: What happened then?

KEN: You mean after that? Um… Nothing really. We went to the neighbours. They called the police.

ROTHKO: What happened to you two?

KEN: State took us. Foster homes. People were nice, actually. They kept us together. But they shuffled us around a lot. We were *rootless*… She's married to a CPA now.

ROTHKO: Rootless?

KEN: Never belonged… Never had a *place*.

ROTHKO: Did they find the guys who did it?

KEN: No. I paint pictures of them sometimes.

Beat.

ROTHKO: You paint pictures of the men who killed your parents?

KEN: Mm. What I imagine them to look like.

ROTHKO: Which is what?

Beat.

KEN: Normal.

Beat.

ROTHKO considers comforting KEN in some way, but doesn't.

He moves away, lights a cigarette.

ROTHKO: When I was a kid in Russia, I saw the Cossacks cutting people up and tossing them into pits… At least I think I remember that, maybe someone told me about it, or I'm just being dramatic, hard to say sometimes.

KEN is relieved that ROTHKO has changed the subject. He continues cleaning up.

KEN: How old were you when you came here?

ROTHKO: Ten. We went to Portland, lived in the ghetto alongside all the other thinky, talky Jews. I was Marcus Rothkowitz then.

KEN: (*Surprised.*) You changed your name?

ROTHKO: My first dealer said he had too many Jewish painters on the books. So Marcus Rothkowitz becomes Mark Rothko. Now nobody knows I'm a Jew!

KEN smiles.

He continues to clean up.

Pause.

KEN: Can I ask you something?

ROTHKO: Can I stop you?

KEN: Are you really scared of black?

ROTHKO: No, I'm really scared of the absence of light.

KEN: Like going blind?

ROTHKO: Like going dead.

KEN: And you equate the color black with death?

ROTHKO: Doesn't everyone?

KEN: I'm asking you.

ROTHKO likes that KEN is pushing back.

ROTHKO: Yes, I equate the color black with the diminution of the life force.

KEN: Black means decay and darkness?

ROTHKO: Doesn't it?

KEN: Because black is the lack of red, if you will.

ROTHKO: Because black is the opposite of red. Not on the spectrum, but in reality.

KEN: I'm talking about in painting.

ROTHKO: Then talk about painting.

KEN: In your pictures the bold colors are the Dionysian element, kept in check by the strict geometric shapes, the Apollonian element. The bright colors are your passion, your will to survive – your 'life force.' But if *black* swallows those bright colors then you lose that excess and extravagance, and what do you have left?

ROTHKO: Go on. I'm fascinated by me.

KEN: (*Undeterred.*) Lose those colors and you have order with
   no content. You have mathematics with no numbers…
   Nothing but empty, arid boxes.

ROTHKO: And trust me, as you get older those colors are
   harder to sustain. The palate fades and we race to catch it
   before it's gone.

KEN: But…

   He stops.

ROTHKO: What?

KEN: Never mind.

ROTHKO: What?

KEN: You'll get mad.

ROTHKO: Me?

KEN: You will.

ROTHKO: And?

KEN: I just think… It's kind of sentimental to equate black
   with death. That seems an antiquated notion. Sort of
   romantic.

ROTHKO: Romantic?

KEN: I mean…not *honest.*

ROTHKO: Really?

KEN: In reality we both know black's a tool, just like ochre or
   magenta. It has no affect. Seeing it as malevolent is a weird
   sort of chromatic anthropomorphising.

ROTHKO: You think so? What about equating white with
   death; like snow?

KEN: That's different. That's just a personal reaction. I'm not building a whole artistic sensibility around it.

ROTHKO: Maybe you should.

They are growing heated.

KEN: I don't think –

ROTHKO: Use your own life, why not?

KEN: It's not that I –

ROTHKO: Unless you're scared of it.

KEN: I'm not scared.

ROTHKO: Go into all that white.

KEN: I'm not scared, it's just self-indulgent.

ROTHKO: If you say so.

KEN: Not all art has to be psychodrama.

ROTHKO: Doesn't it?

KEN: No.

ROTHKO: You paint pictures of the men who killed your parents.

KEN: That's not *all* I paint.

ROTHKO: Maybe it should be. Then maybe you'd understand what black is.

KEN: Back to that.

ROTHKO: Always.

KEN: At least equating white with death isn't so predictable.

ROTHKO: I'm predictable now?

KEN: Kind of.

ROTHKO: Dishonest and predictable.

KEN: Come on, a painter gets older and the color black starts to infuse his work therefore, the cliché declension goes, he's depressed, he's fearing death, he's losing touch, he's losing relevance, he's saying goodbye.

ROTHKO: That's a cliché except for when it's not.

KEN: But it's not *true.*

ROTHKO: So now you know truth?

KEN: Look at Van Gogh; his last pictures are all color. He goes out and paints the most ecstatic yellows and blues known to man – then shoots himself… Or Matisse, his last works were nothing but great shocks of primary colors.

ROTHKO: You admire those colors.

KEN: Absolutely.

ROTHKO: Why?

KEN: Well, Matisse…he was dying, he knew he was dying, but still he was Matisse. When he got too ill to hold a paint brush he used scissors, cutting up paper and making collages. He never gave up. On his deathbed he was still organizing the color patterns on the ceiling. He had to be who he was.

ROTHKO: And you think *I'm* the romantic! Can't you do any better than that?

He continues, angry and derisive:

ROTHKO: Matisse the Dying Hero, struggling with his last puny gasp to create that final masterpiece… And Jackson Pollock the Beautiful Doomed Youth, dying like Chatterton in his classic Pieta-pose… And Van Gogh, of course Van Gogh, trotted out on all occasions, the ubiquitous symbol for everything, Van Gogh the Misunderstood Martyr – You *insult* these men by reducing them to your own adolescent stereotypes. Grapple with them, yes. Argue with them, always. But don't think you *understand* them. Don't think you have *captured* them. *They are beyond you.*

He moves away, then stops.

ROTHKO: Spend a *lifetime* with them and you might get a moment of insight into their pain… Until then, allow them their grandeur in silence.

ROTHKO returns to studying his central painting.

ROTHKO: Silence is so accurate.

Pause.

ROTHKO seems oblivious to KEN.

KEN continues to clean up for a moment.

Then he stops, looks at his own painting, wrapped in brown paper.

Then he looks at ROTHKO.

KEN unobtrusively picks up his painting and exits briefly. He returns without the painting.

KEN: We need some coffee. Mind if I go out?

ROTHKO: Go on.

KEN gets some money from the coffee can in which they keep petty cash.

He starts to go.

ROTHKO stops him:

ROTHKO: Wait.

ROTHKO looks at him.

ROTHKO: In the National Gallery in London there's a picture by Rembrandt called 'Belshazzar's Feast'… It's an Old Testament story from Daniel: Belshazzar, King of Babylon, is giving a feast and he blasphemes, so a divine hand appears and writes some Hebrew words on the wall as a warning… In the painting these words pulsate from the dark canvas like something miraculous. Rembrandt's Hebrew was atrocious, as you can imagine, but he wrote 'Mene, Mene, Tekel, Upharsin.'… 'You have been weighed in the balance and have been found wanting.'

Beat.

ROTHKO: That's what black is to me… What is it to you?

Beat.

SCENE FOUR

KEN is alone, building a wooden canvas stretcher/frame. He is a good carpenter.

A Chet Baker jazz record plays on the phonograph.

He works quietly.

Beat.

Then the sound of a slamming door from outside surprises him.

ROTHKO rages in, flinging off his overcoat and hat.

ROTHKO: THEY'RE TRYING TO KILL ME! I swear to God they're trying to kill me! Those prosaic insects! Those presumptuous, counter-jumping, arriviste SONS-OF-BITCHES! – These are same goddamn walls where I hang! You appreciate that?! *My* gallery! *My* walls! Polluted now beyond sanitation, beyond hygiene, like the East River, choked with garbage, all that superficial, meaningless sewage right up there on the wall! The same sacred space of de Kooning and Motherwell and Smith and Newman and Pollock and…

He stops.

ROTHKO: What is this music?

KEN: Chet Baker.

ROTHKO: Just when I thought this day couldn't get worse…

KEN: It's jazz.

ROTHKO: Like I care. When you pay the rent, you can pick the records.

KEN takes the record off.

ROTHKO fumes.

Beat.

KEN: So…how did you like the exhibit?

ROTHKO is not amused.

He lights a cigarette.

ROTHKO: (*Seriously.*) These young artists are out to murder me.

KEN: That's kind of extreme.

ROTHKO: But not inaccurate.

KEN: You think Jasper Johns is trying to murder you?

ROTHKO: Yes.

Beat.

KEN: What about Frank Stella?

ROTHKO: Yes.

KEN: Robert Rauschenberg?

ROTHKO: Yes.

KEN: Roy Lichtenstein?

ROTHKO: Which one is he?

KEN: Comic books.

ROTHKO: Yes.

Beat. Then the coup de grace:

KEN: Andy Warhol?

ROTHKO doesn't even answer.

KEN: You sound like an old man.

ROTHKO: I am an old man.

KEN: Not that old.

ROTHKO: Today, I'm old.

KEN: If you say so.

KEN goes back to working on the stretcher.

ROTHKO gets a Scotch.

ROTHKO: My point is… People like me… My contemporaries, my colleagues… Those painters who came up with me. We all had one thing in common… We understood the importance of seriousness.

Beat.

KEN: You're too much.

ROTHKO: What?

KEN: You heard me.

ROTHKO turns and really looks at him.

This challenging tone is new from KEN.

ROTHKO: What did you say to me?

KEN: Who are you to assume they're not serious?

ROTHKO: Look at their work.

KEN: I have.

ROTHKO: Not like you usually look at things, like an overeager undergraduate –

KEN: *I have.*

ROTHKO: Then what do you see?

KEN: Never mind.

ROTHKO: No. You look at them, what do you see?

KEN: This moment, right now.

ROTHKO: In all those flags and comic books and soup cans?

KEN: This moment, right now, and a little bit tomorrow.

ROTHKO: And you think that's good?

KEN: It's neither good nor bad, but it's what people want.

ROTHKO: Exactly my point.

KEN: So art shouldn't be popular at all now?

ROTHKO: It shouldn't *only* be popular.

KEN: You may not like it, but nowadays as many people are genuinely moved by Frank Stella as by Mark Rothko.

ROTHKO: That's nonsense.

KEN: Don't think so.

ROTHKO: You know the problem with those painters? It's *exactly* what you said: they are painting for this moment right now. And that's all. It's nothing but zeitgeist art. Completely temporal, completely disposable, like Kleenex, like –

KEN: Like Campbell's soup, like comic books –

ROTHKO: You really think Andy Warhol will be hanging in museums in a hundred years? Alongside the Bruegels and the Vermeers?

KEN: He's hanging alongside Rothko now.

ROTHKO: Because those goddamn galleries will do anything for money – cater to any wicked taste. That's *business*, young man, not art!

KEN approaches. Not backing down.

KEN: You ever get tired of telling people what art is?

ROTHKO: No, not ever. Until they listen. Better you should tell me? Fuck off.

KEN: You're just mad because the Barbarians are at the gate. And, whattaya know, people seem to like the Barbarians.

ROTHKO: Of course they *like* them. That's the goddamn point! You know what people *like*? Happy, bright colors. They want things to be *pretty*. They want things to be *beautiful* – Jesus Christ, when someone tells me one of my pictures is 'beautiful' I want to vomit!

KEN: What's wrong with –?

ROTHKO: (*Explodes.*) 'Pretty.' 'Beautiful.' 'Nice.' '*Fine.*' That's our life now! Everything's 'fine.' We put on the funny nose and glasses and slip on the banana peel and the TV makes everything happy and everyone's laughing all the time, it's all so goddamn funny, it's our constitutional right to be amused all the time, isn't it? We're a smirking nation, living under the tyranny of 'fine.' How are you? Fine. How was your day? Fine. How are you feeling? Fine. How did you like the painting? Fine. Want some dinner? Fine… Well, let me tell you, *everything is not fine*!

He spins to his paintings.

ROTHKO: HOW ARE YOU?!… HOW WAS YOUR DAY?!… HOW ARE YOU FEELING? Conflicted. Nuanced. Troubled. Diseased. Doomed. I am not fine. We are not fine. We are anything but fine… Look at these pictures. *Look at them*! You see the dark rectangle, like a doorway, an aperture, yes, but it's also a gaping mouth letting out a silent howl of something feral and

foul and primal and REAL. Not nice. Not fine. *Real.*
A moan of rapture. Something divine or damned.
Something immortal, not comic books or soup cans,
something beyond me and beyond now. And whatever
it is, it's not pretty and it's not fine... (*He grabs KEN's
heart.*) ... I AM HERE TO STOP YOUR HEART, YOU
UNDERSTAND THAT?!... (*He slaps KEN's forehead.*) – I
AM HERE TO MAKE YOU THINK!... I AM NOT
HERE TO MAKE PRETTY PICTURES!

A long beat.

ROTHKO roams, disturbed, trying to recover his equilibrium.

KEN hasn't moved.

KEN: So said the Cubist, the second before you stomped him
to death.

ROTHKO stops, looks at him.

KEN: 'Tragic, really, to grow superfluous in your own
lifetime'... Right?... 'The child must banish the father.
Respect him, but kill him'... Isn't that what you said?...
You guys went after the Cubists and Surrealists and, boy,
did you love it. And now your time has come and you
don't want to go. Well, exit stage left, Rothko. Because Pop
Art has banished Abstract Expressionism... I only pray to
God they have more generosity of spirit than you do, and
allow you some dignity as you go.

He glances around at the paintings.

KEN: Consider: The last gasp of a dying race... Futility.

Beat.

KEN: Don't worry; you can always sign menus for money.

ROTHKO: How dare you?

KEN: Do you know where I live?

ROTHKO: (*Confused.*) What?

KEN: Do you know where I live in the city?

ROTHKO: No…

KEN: Uptown? Downtown? Brooklyn?

ROTHKO: No.

KEN: You know if I'm married?

ROTHKO: What?

KEN: You know if I'm married? Dating? Queer? Anything?

ROTHKO: No. Why should –?

KEN: *Two years* I've been working here. Eight hours a day, five days a week and you know nothing about me. You ever once asked me to dinner? Maybe come to your house?

ROTHKO: What is –?

KEN: You know I'm a painter, don't you?

ROTHKO: I suppose.

KEN: No, answer me, you know I'm a painter?

ROTHKO: Yes.

KEN: Have you ever once asked to look at my work?

ROTHKO: Why should I?

KEN: Why should you?

ROTHKO: You're an *employee.* This is about me. Everything here is about me. You don't like that; leave… Is that what this is all about? Baby feels wounded Daddy didn't pat him on the head? Mommy didn't hug you today?

KEN: Stop it –

ROTHKO: Don't blame me, I didn't kill them.

KEN: Stop it –!

ROTHKO: Go find a psychiatrist and quit whining to me about it, your neediness bores me –

KEN: (*Explodes.*) Bores you?! *Bores you*?! – Christ almighty, trying working for *you* for a living! – The talking-talking-talking-jesus-christ-won't-he-ever-shut-up titanic self-absorption of the man! You stand there trying to look so deep when you're nothing but a solipsistic bully with your grandiose self-importance and lectures and arias and let's-look-at-the-fucking-canvas-for-another-few-weeks-let's-not-fucking-paint-let's-just-look. And the *pretension*! Jesus Christ, the *pretension*! I can't imagine any other painter in the history of art ever tried so hard to be SIGNIFICANT!

KEN roams angrily.

KEN: You know, not everything has to be so goddamn IMPORTANT all the time! Not every painting has to rip your guts out and expose your soul! Not everyone wants art that actually HURTS! Sometimes you just want a fucking still life or landscape or soup can or comic book! Which you might learn if you ever actually left your goddamn hermetically-sealed *submarine* here with all the windows closed and no natural light – BECAUSE NATURAL LIGHT ISN'T GOOD ENOUGH FOR YOU!

ROTHKO lights a cigarette. He continues to stare at KEN.

KEN: But then *nothing* is ever good enough for you! Not even the people who buy your pictures! Museums are nothing but mausoleums, galleries are run by pimps and swindlers, and art collectors are nothing but shallow social-climbers. So who *is* good enough to own your art?! Anyone?!

He stops, slows, realizing.

KEN: Or maybe the real question is: who's good enough to even *see* your art?… Is it just possible *no one* is worthy to look at your paintings?… That's it, isn't it?… We have all been 'weighed in the balance and have been found wanting.'

He approaches ROTHKO.

KEN: You say you spend your life in search of real 'human beings,' people who can look at your pictures with compassion. But in your heart you no longer believe those people exist… So you lose faith… So you lose hope… So black swallows red.

Beat.

KEN is standing right before ROTHKO.

KEN: My friend, I don't think you'd recognize a real human being if he were standing right in front of you.

Pause.

ROTHKO's stern and uncompromising Old Testament glare makes KEN uneasy.

KEN's resolve starts to crumble.

He moves away.

KEN: Never mind.

ROTHKO: Don't give up so easy!

KEN: It's not a game.

ROTHKO: You do make one salient point, though not the one you think.

KEN: Naturally.

ROTHKO: I do get depressed when I think how people are going to see my pictures. If they're going to be unkind… Selling a picture is like sending a blind child into a room full of razor blades. It's going to get hurt and it's never been hurt before, it doesn't know what hurt is.

He looks around at the mural paintings.

ROTHKO: That's why I'm looking to do something different with these ones. They're less vulnerable somehow, more robust, some hues from the earth even to give them strength. And they're not *alone*. They're a series, they'll always have each other for companionship and protection... And most important they're going into a *place* created just for them. A place of reflection and safety...

KEN: A place of contemplation...

ROTHKO: Yes...

KEN: A place with no distractions...

ROTHKO: Yes...

KEN: A sacred space...

ROTHKO: Yes...

KEN: A chapel...

ROTHKO: Yes...

KEN: Like the Four Seasons restaurant.

ROTHKO stops.

KEN shakes his head.

KEN: At least Andy Warhol gets the joke.

ROTHKO: No, you don't understand –

KEN: It's a fancy restaurant in a big high rise owned by a rich corporation, what don't I understand?

ROTHKO: You don't understand my intention –

KEN: Your intention is immaterial. Unless you're going to stand there for the rest of your life next to the pictures giving lectures – which you'd probably enjoy. The art has to speak for itself, yes?

ROTHKO: Yes, but –

KEN: Just admit your hypocrisy: the High Priest of Modern Art is painting a wall in the Temple of Consumption. You rail against commercialism in art, but pal, you're taking the money.

ROTHKO: I –

KEN: Sure, you can try to kid yourself you're making a holy place of contemplative awe, but in reality you're just decorating another dining room for the super-rich and these things – (*He gestures to the murals.*) – are nothing but the world's most expensive *overmantles*.

The words sting ROTHKO.

Beat.

ROTHKO: Why do you think I took this commission?

KEN: It appealed to your vanity.

ROTHKO: How so?

KEN: They could have gone to de Kooning, they went to you… It's the flashiest mural commission since the Sistine Chapel.

ROTHKO: You would have turned it down?

KEN: In a second.

ROTHKO: Easy for you to say.

KEN: You know what it is? It's your Oldsmobile convertible… Come on, you don't need the money. You don't need the publicity. Why make yourself a hypocrite for the Seagram Corporation?

ROTHKO: I didn't enter into this capriciously, you know. I *thought* about it.

KEN: No kidding.

ROTHKO: And of course it appealed to my vanity, I'm a human being too. But still I hesitated… The very same thoughts: is it corrupt? is it immoral? just feeding the whims of the bourgeoisie? should I do it?… I'm still thinking what the murals might look like when I take a trip to Europe. I happened to go to Michelangelo's Medici Library in Florence. You been there?

KEN: No.

ROTHKO: When you go, be sure to find the staircase, it's hidden away. It's a tiny vestibule, like a vault it's so cramped, but it goes up for three stories. Michelangelo embraced this claustrophobia and created false doors and windows all the way up the walls, rectangles in rich reds and browns... Well, that was it... He achieved just the kind of feeling I was after for the Four Seasons. He makes the viewer feel he is trapped in a room where all the doors and windows are bricked up, so all he can do is butt his head against the wall forever.

He turns to KEN:

ROTHKO: I know that place is where the richest bastards in New York will come to feed and show off... And I hope to ruin the appetite of every son-of-a-bitch who eats there.

KEN: You mention this to the Seagram's people?

ROTHKO: It would be a compliment if they turned the murals down. They won't.

KEN thinks about this.

Beat.

ROTHKO: You wanna drink?

KEN: (*Surprised.*) Sure.

ROTHKO pours two glasses of Scotch. He gives one to KEN.

Beat.

KEN: I don't know...

ROTHKO: What?

KEN: I don't know that I believe you.

ROTHKO: About what?

KEN: (*Referring to the murals.*) Them – This malicious intent of yours. The old lion still roaring, still trying to provoke, to be relevant, stick it to the bourgeoisie – it doesn't scan.

ROTHKO: Too romantic for you?

KEN: Too cruel to them. Your paintings aren't weapons. You would never do that to them, never reduce them like that. Maybe you started the commission thinking that way but... then art happened... You couldn't help it, that's what you do. So now you're stuck. You've painted yourself into a corner, you should forgive the expression.

KEN moves away.

ROTHKO remains standing, unsure.

ROTHKO: No, you're wrong.

KEN doesn't respond.

ROTHKO: Their power will transcend the setting. Working together, moving in rhythm, whispering to each other, they will still create a *place.*

His words sound hollow.

ROTHKO: You think I'm kidding myself.

KEN doesn't answer.

ROTHKO: You think it's all an act of monumental self-delusion... Answer me.

ROTHKO stares at KEN.

ROTHKO: Answer me.

KEN: Yes.

ROTHKO continues to stare intensely at KEN.

Beat.

KEN: I'm fired, aren't I?

ROTHKO: Fired?… This is the first time you've existed.

ROTHKO drains his Scotch, takes his hat and overcoat.

ROTHKO: See you tomorrow.

He goes.

A beat as KEN stands, a little mystified.

Then he moves forward to study the central painting.

He stands, glass of Scotch in one hand, tilting his head, very Rothko-like.

SCENE FIVE

The room is almost in darkness.

Classical music plays loudly from the phonograph.

ROTHKO is slumped awkwardly on the floor, gazing up at the central picture.

There is a bottle of Scotch and a bucket of red paint next to him. He has been drinking for a long time, but is not drunk. He can barely be seen in the gloom.

A long beat.

KEN enters.

KEN: (*Over the music.*) CAN I LOWER THE MUSIC?

ROTHKO doesn't respond. KEN lowers the volume.

Then he turns on some more lights:

He stops —

It is a shocking sight —

ROTHKO's hands and arms are dripping with red.

It's paint, but looks just like blood.

KEN thinks he has slashed his wrists.

KEN: Jesus Christ —!

He hurries to ROTHKO, panicked.

KEN: What did you do?!… (*Realizes it is paint.*) … Oh Christ, it's paint!

ROTHKO: I was going to work.

KEN: Obviously… Jesus Christ… You want a towel or something? Maybe a paint brush?

KEN gets a bucket of water. He cleans ROTHKO's hands.

Beat.

ROTHKO: I went there.

KEN: What?

ROTHKO: The Four Seasons.

KEN: Ah.

ROTHKO: After our 'chat' yesterday… I went there last night. For dinner.

KEN: Ah.

ROTHKO: It's been open a couple weeks now, thought I should finally take a look…

KEN: And…?

ROTHKO pulls himself up.

He stands there, unsteady. Stares forward, lost in thought.

Beat.

KEN: What do you see?

ROTHKO shakes his head.

KEN: What do you see?

Beat.

ROTHKO: (*Reliving it.*) You go in from 52nd… Then you go up some stairs to the restaurant… You *hear* the room before you see it. Glasses clinking, silverware, voices, hushed here but building as you get closer, it's a desperate sound, like forced gaiety at gunpoint… You go in, feel underdressed, feel fat, feel too goddamn Jewish for this place. Give your name. Pretty hostess gives you a look that says: 'I know who you are and I'm not impressed, we get millionaires in here, pal, for all I care you might as well be some schmuck painting marionettes in Tijuana.' She snaps for the Maitre 'D who snaps for the captain who snaps for the head waiter who brings you through the crowd to your table, heads turning, everyone looking at everyone else all the time, like predators – who are you? what are you worth? do I need to fear you? do I need to acquire you?… Wine guy comes, speaks French, you feel inadequate, you obviously don't understand, he doesn't care. You embarrass yourself ordering something expensive to impress the wine guy. He goes, unimpressed. You look around. Everyone else seems to belong here: men with elegant silver hair and women with capes and gloves. Someone else in a uniform brings you the menu. It's things you never heard of: suckling pig under glass, quail eggs in aspic. You are lost. And then… you can't help it, you start hearing what people are saying around you… Which is the worst of all…

ROTHKO pulls himself up.

He stands there, unsteady. It's disquieting: the dripping red paint really does look like blood.

ROTHKO: The voices… It's the chatter of monkeys and the barking of jackals. It's not human… And everyone's clever and everyone's laughing and everyone's investing in this or that and everyone's on this charity board or that and everyone's jetting off here or there and no one looks at anything and no one thinks about anything and all they do is chatter and bark and eat and the knives and forks click and clack and the words cut and the teeth snap and snarl.

Beat.

He spreads his arms, taking in his murals:

ROTHKO: And in that place – *there* – will live my paintings for all time.

Beat.

He finally turns to KEN:

ROTHKO: I wonder… Do you think they'll ever forgive me?

KEN: They're only paintings.

KEN stares at him.

It's like a challenge.

ROTHKO holds his gaze.

Pause.

And then ROTHKO seems to come to some decision.

He gets angry.

He nods.

He goes to the cluttered counter and finds the phone. He looks up.

ROTHKO: (*Referring to the phonograph.*) Turn that off, would ya?

KEN turns off the record player as ROTHKO dials.

ROTHKO: (*On phone.*) Mister Philip Johnson, please. This is Mark Rothko on the line… (*he waits, then.*) … Philip, this is Rothko. Listen, I went to the restaurant last night and lemme tell you, anyone who eats that kind of food for that kind of money in that kind of joint will never look at a painting of mine. I'm sending the money back and I'm keeping the pictures. No offence. This is how it goes. Good luck to ya, buddy.

He hangs up with a joyous finality.

KEN: (*Proud.*) Now…now you are Mark Rothko.

ROTHKO: Only poorer.

KEN: Having money doesn't make you wealthy.

ROTHKO: It helps though.

KEN: Well, this is a day for the books, we'll have to –

ROTHKO: You're fired.

KEN stops.

KEN: What?

ROTHKO: You're fired.

Beat.

KEN stares at him. He can't believe it.

KEN: Why?

ROTHKO busies himself organizing something.

ROTHKO: Doesn't matter.

KEN: It does.

ROTHKO: Write down your address, I'll send your final check.

KEN: You owe me an explanation.

ROTHKO: I don't owe you anything –

KEN pursues. ROTHKO tries to avoid him. The conflict builds:

KEN: Two years and you expect me to walk out, just like that?

ROTHKO: You want a retirement party?

KEN: I want a reason.

ROTHKO: None of your business.

KEN: I want a reason.

ROTHKO: Look, you're too goddamn needy, all right? I don't need it. I don't need your need. Since you're seven you're looking for a home – well this isn't it, and I'm not your father. Your father's dead, remember? Sorry, but that's it.

KEN isn't deterred.

KEN: Come on, Doctor Freud. You can do better. *Why?*

ROTHKO: I told you.

KEN: Why?

ROTHKO: Because I don't need an assistant –

KEN: Bullshit.

ROTHKO: Because you talk too much –

KEN: So do you.

ROTHKO: Because you have lousy taste –

KEN: Bullshit.

ROTHKO: Because I'm sick of you –

KEN: Bullshit –

ROTHKO spins on him, points to the outside:

ROTHKO: *Because your life is out there!*

Beat.

ROTHKO: Listen, kid, you don't need to spend any more time with me. You need to find your contemporaries and make your own world, your own life… You need to get *out there* now, into the thick of it, shake your fist at them, talk their ear off…

ROTHKO steps close, touches KEN.

ROTHKO: *Make them look.*

KEN is moved.

ROTHKO continues with quiet emotion.

ROTHKO: When I was your age, art was a lonely thing: no galleries, no collecting, no critics, no money. We didn't have mentors. We didn't have parents. We were alone. But it was a great time, because we had nothing to lose and a vision to gain.

Beat.

ROTHKO: Okay?

KEN: Okay.

Beat.

KEN: Thank you.

ROTHKO: Make something new.

KEN gathers his things, starts to go.

He stops at the door.

He turns back. He takes in the paintings and ROTHKO one last time.

ROTHKO: (*Referring to the central painting.*) What do you see?

KEN looks at the painting.

But then he looks at ROTHKO.

Beat.

KEN: Red.

Beat.

KEN goes to the phonograph and puts on a record.

Classical music plays.

KEN goes.

ROTHKO seems a little lost.

He moves to the central painting and stares at it.

Pause.

ROTHKO stands alone.

The End.